HELP!
I HAVE AN ALIEN IN MY HOUSE!

HELP!
I HAVE AN ALIEN
IN MY HOUSE!

~

GIRL, LET'S TALK!

EVE IKUENOBE-OTAIGBE

iUniverse, Inc.
New York   Bloomington

Help! I have an Alien in my house!
Girl, let's talk!

iUniverse books may be ordered through booksellers or by contacting:

iUniverse
1663 Liberty Drive
Bloomington, IN 47403
www.iuniverse.com
1-800-Authors (1-800-288-4677)

ISBN: 978-1-4502-6516-4 (sc)
ISBN: 978-1-4502-6517-1 (ebk)

Printed in the United States of America

iUniverse rev. date: 11/01/2010

Acknowledgment

Thanks to the select Editorial Board.

Dr. Francisca Oboh-Ikuenobe, Dr. Josephine Ediale,

Ms. Lillian Asoera, Mrs. Deborah Okosun, Dr. Bosede Ojo,

Dr. Omolara Otaigbe, Mrs. Emilia Odunayo-Olusesi, Dr. Omegbai Uriri.

Thanks to Darlene King: for all graphics and pictures.

Thanks to TJ Nanna for APA formatting.

Thanks to the many people who participated in the interviews and
survey exercises.

Most special appreciation to my wonderful husband, for being my
Rock of Gibraltar.

And to my wonderful children, for being God's gift to me, my joy,
blessing and greatest inspiration.

Finally, to the young orphan girls who fate destined me to meet,
who adopted me as mother and asked me to teach them about
becoming women of substance: You are the reason this came alive.

Foreword

"Help! I have an Alien in my house" presents a first hand, eye opening experience and a navigation tool for the teenage years and beyond. It is an amazing book as the author skillfully addresses issues and conditions associated with teenage girls in a language suited for easy comprehension, identification of the subject matter and an incorporation of her personal experiences to establish credibility,

The author is motivated to write a book that educates and entertains young girls about capacity building, communication skills, cultural and societal challenges, taking ownership of their sexuality by embracing physical changes, adapting to corresponding emotional and psychological changes associated with it and emerging as respectable young women able to hold their own and contribute positively to the development of the society.

This book provides a road map to a successful teenage life and beyond. It should be on every teenager's book shelf. Enjoy reading it!

Dr. Eugenia 'Busola George

<u>Reader's comments....</u>

An interesting segment of this book is the teenage text language (shorthand and acronym) which is an absolute for parents and the incorporation of personal testimonies from teenagers and their mothers.

It is obviously a strong desire for this author in writing this book to minister, mentor and educate young women all over. Her desire is to foster an understanding while relieving stress for both parents and daughter as they encounter this journey together.

"Help! I have an Alien in my house"... makes you realize that if you take the time to understand and empower, the teenage girl is a treasure to have.

Societal expectations of girls in comparison to boys are painfully different.

We must invest time, tools and materials to empower them to navigate this critical period in their lives seamlessly. This book provides a road map to a successful teenage life and beyond.

Preamble

Who or what is an alien? The online dictionary describes an alien as *"any being or thing foreign to the environment in which it now exists 3. (In science fiction) OR a being from another world, sometimes specifically an extraterrestrial."*

"Help! I have an Alien in my house!" What comes to mind is E.T, or very strange creatures that come from another planet or space. They come and invade the world as humans know it and are eerie, unfathomable, and possessing strange powers.

Indeed, parents and teens often view each other from the prism that they are aliens. Teenagers view adults like they must be from Mars! And parents are so totally convinced that their children are U.F.Os.

Hopefully, this book will help to unravel the issues teenage girls deal with in their own world. It is meant to be as personally comfortable as possible for the readers, informative, educational and entertaining. It deals with various issues relating to teenage girls from the anatomical, psychological and mental perspectives. With the new wave in technology, it addresses the influence of social networks and the internet.

"Help! I have an Alien in my house" empowers young women to take charge and control of their lives. It allows them realize that what they are dealing with or their conflicts and dilemmas are not strange or foreign, but cuts across global lines. This book brings an awareness and preparedness for the life ahead, what the future holds for young women and how to be ready for it.

Introduction

A high percentage of parents, mostly those from certain cultural orientations are reluctant to discuss certain sexually-related issues with their children, particularly daughters. Fear of promiscuity, the right timing and ability to tackle the sensitive subject matter are some reasons given. Unfortunately, more often than not, when parents do decide to have that dialogue, it is usually too late. Parents are alarmed to find that their children have obtained the information through trial and error, from their peers or other external sources. As the teenage years come, it seems that there is a metamorphosis of children such that parents seem not to recognize the emerging "alien."

Communication and understanding are fundamental elements that authors agree need to be present between any two parties and this theory affects parents and teenagers or men and women. Chinwezu, author of 1990" **The Anatomy of the Female Power** and John Gray, author of 1992 "**Men are from Mars, Women are from Venus**" are two authors that try to explain the differences in the mental and psychological makeup of men and women. It is a complex maze and so, it is not surprising that through the years, the sexes still have difficulties understanding each other.

1

Let me stop and say first, I love being a woman! We are gifted with intuition, multi-tasking capabilities and I love the way we as women express ourselves. Imagine this... a group of women, hands on the hip, eyes blazing with excitement, hearts in trepidation of some very "juicy" information about to spill out! There is the high anticipation of laughter, resolutions.... So, yes, this is how girlfriends and confidants feel when they talk in hush tones and whispers, as the world of intrigue, mystery and secrecy opens up in truth, honesty and candor.

For teenage girls, same rules apply. Unfortunately, once an adult comes into a teenage gathering, the open line of dialogue or communication flow is interrupted. Why? It seems to teenagers that adults are aliens, simply "strange" "ignorant" and totally bereft of understanding. Teenagers crave security in someone who can be open, trustworthy, objective, caring, and sensitive, while being honest, understanding and able to let them know where and how to draw the line. Teenage girl, you need to know that these older folks, you know, like mum and dad, were once teenagers too! (I know that is so hard to imagine) So let us assume we are in that little circle, and you, my young ladies, between the ages of 13-19 are right here, then we are about to embark on the most fulfilling expedition together.

<u>Reflection</u>

It is amazing how the world has evolved! Today, information is readily accessible to young girls via the internet and technology in most advanced countries. Growing up in the 1960s in Africa, this was not so. Sadly, easy access still eludes those in developing nations. Yours truly was raised in very "Catholic Christian" home in Nigeria, Africa. It was typical for most of our parents (the generation of fathers/mothers who are now 70 years and over) not to discuss certain "taboo" topics with us. To make it worse, many of us between the ages of 9-11years were "carted" off to boarding secondary schools. (Equivalent of 6th-12th grades).

We were welcomed by straight-faced nuns all covered from head-to-toe in white dresses in this remote gothic convent many miles away from civilization: I felt I was thrown into this world. It was impossible that this was not a depiction of medieval drama. My school was a well-known strict Catholic all-girl boarding school where there were too many rules to live by, authoritatively dictated by a very old, rusty bell. The reverend sisters and mothers also taught us that "girls should be seen not heard" and so we learned not to raise our voices. Our lives were centered and dictated by the Holy Mass, the Novenas, and the faithful recital of the Rosary. We were very obviously sheltered from the outside world. There was no health or sex education and we got into our teenage lives with daily shocks about our developing bodies, body images, womanhood and of course, boys. This meant we were totally unprepared for the changes we were about to undergo.

That was how it was then.

Fast forward...light years ahead. A huge contrast... a more aggressive media system has come to play a huge role in creating awareness for young girls and in ways, giving a firsthand lesson to today's young girls. The hassle and stress of the West keeps some parents so preoccupied that they forget to have that all important "talk" with their daughters and the internet becomes the primary source of information.

1.
—
Physical

There are so many phases or ways in the transition from childhood to puberty. And as a young girl, you must begin to realize that you will be changing, not only physically, but psychologically as well. As children, at least before eight years of age, we do not take note or seriously consider the difference between the male and female body and when we do; it is purely out of curiosity. This is because in some cultures, there is no marked difference in treatment based on gender. Actually, in some African countries, all children regardless of gender, sleep together, play together and no one cares about their differences.

These are questions you hear from curious children:

Why do I have this, and you don't?

Why do boys have penis and girls don't?

Why is mummy's stomach big and she goes to the hospital and comes home with a baby...how did it get there? How did it get out?

Onset of Puberty.

What is puberty? According to the free online dictionary,

"it is the development of humans and other primates marked by the development of **secondary sex characteristics**, including menarche in females. In humans, puberty occurs at the onset of adolescence, between the ages of about 11 and 14 in girls and 13 and 16 in boys."

When children get to between 8 and 10 years, noticeable physical changes start to present themselves and the questions commence. Biological changes in the body are the first physical signs of a girl's maturity. These changes are caused by hormones.

The most important hormones are made in the ovaries and are the two main female sex hormones: estrogen and progesterone. The ovaries also produce some of the male hormone, testosterone.

(yes.....that is why some women grow beards, moustache, hairy chest and have deep voices while some men have breasts and feminine features!....)

During puberty, estrogen prompts:

1. Breast development
2. Maturity of the uterus (womb)
3. Maturity of the Fallopian tubes (transportation channel of eggs to the womb).

This hormone also plays a role in the growth spurt and re-apportions the depository of fat on the hips, buttocks and thighs.

It is important for you to realize that everyone starts puberty at different ages. Some scholars and researchers say the age for onset of puberty has been declining in recent times because of better nutrition.

For some girls, puberty starts between ages of 8 and 13, some younger and some older. Many girls don't start puberty until age 13 and so if you are worried that you have not begun to see any changes by this age, you can speak to an adult who you are comfortable talking to. And if you get to be much older than 13 and puberty has not begun (known as 'delayed puberty'), it is a good idea to speak to a doctor to make sure there are no underlying health problems. And you may not experience all the signs of puberty at this age.

The body changes with puberty: the most obvious being breasts.

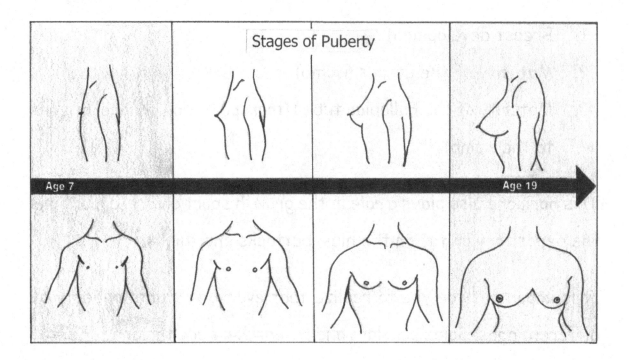

They will start to itch and grow. This itching usually stops when the breasts stop growing. Breasts grow as differently as we all do. They are usually unequal in size: one usually bigger. Some may remain small for life, while others become very big. It is amazing that in adult life, women still have issues about their breasts, often going into all sorts of surgery and medications. This is mainly because of the media portrayal of ideal breast shape and size. What each of us has is a unique pair of breasts designed, molded and formed just for you.

<u>Reflection.</u>

As a teenager in high school, breast size was a fascination for me. I questioned the issue of sizes and finally rationalized that all these breasts would all grow up soon, some day, to be the same.

Ideal image shape affects girls when growing up. How do you feel when all your friends start using a bra and you haven't? And kids can cruelly make jokes and fun of each other's physical traits! It gets worse when the boys start making fun of you, either calling you flat-chest or water-melons! That just beats your self-confidence, doesn't it? Due to this, there were all sorts of miracle-wonder tricks we tried to use to make the breasts grow!

Please, leave the breasts alone. Trust me, when you start nursing or breast feeding, those breasts may go to "sleep" or "lie down flat" permanently!! And it is all in the joy of motherhood!

Surgery becomes the answer but please be conscious of the consequences. Many women have spoken out about the disastrous result of breast augmentation.

Down the belly button are the hips which get wider and rounder. You know those models you see straddling the runway? Their hands are always on the hips. They walk fluidly, swinging the hips from left to right that the hips have taken on an aesthetic identity of their own!

Reflection.

A funny incident occurred when I was about 12 years old. Talk about myths and legends, even from the professionals!

I had to have my appendix removed. As I lay down on the theatre bed, the surgeon looked down at me and his words to the nurse as I struggled though the enveloping waves of anaesthesia were "She has such narrow hips: she is so thin, childbirth would be a big problem." This statement remained buried in my subconscious but reared its head when I got married and pregnant with my first child. I was worried that the baby would be breeched or I would have serious complications because of my "narrow hips".

So, I asked my OBGYN (obstetrics & gynecologist) if I would need a caesarean section/surgery to deliver my baby. He was totally puzzled. I did not tell him the genesis of this question in order not to sound ignorant. I eventually had four lovely healthy children: naturally and without complications too.

The moral of this lesson? As a young girl, your body keeps developing. And a word to healthcare providers...do be careful what you say within ear shot of patients!

So what role does the hip play? The hip bones are called the pelvis bones and are the birth canal through which a baby passes. According to Wikipedia, before puberty, the pelvis can consist of more than ten bones, which eventually fuse into the three main bones. The name "Pelvis" is said to originate from the Latin word meaning "Basin" and the pelvis does look like a basin, doesn't it?

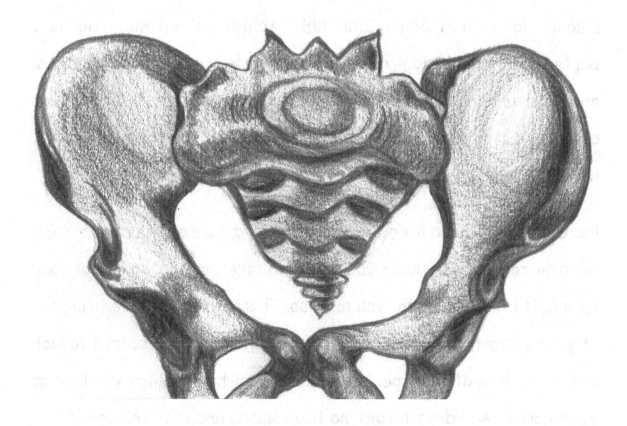

As a woman gets ready to give birth, that hormone, Progesterone, is released to relax the ligaments between joints. The body makes a passageway (the pelvis) so that the passenger (the baby) can come out by creating the diameter large enough for the baby to negotiate during labor. See the importance of the pelvis and why my surgeon thought I was in trouble?

These same hormone, Progesterone, is responsible for the growth of the outward sex organs called 'genitals" and internally called the reproductive organs. All genitals naturally vary in appearance so they will not all look like the "ideal" genitals represented in pictures.

Please, don't start going "uhhhhhh, Ahhhhhhh" on me. This is a perfectly natural biological feature and girls; we are being practical and for real here, ok! If you have not done this before, I suggest you do this as soon as possible. It is important for you to know *exactly* how YOU look *there*.

Here is what you need to do. Before your period, take off your underwear, get a mirror, put it between your legs and take a very good look at your vagina. It is necessary for you to do so. This is the most beautiful part of your anatomy and you must never be ashamed of or scared to look at it. Boys look at their penis every day, so why shouldn't you look at your vagina? And don't forget, no two vaginas are ever the same!

Typically what do we see when we look in the mirror?

Female Sex Organs

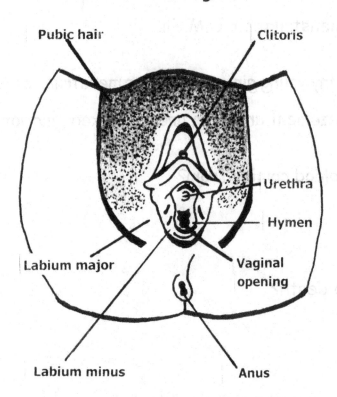

Between the legs there are three small holes. In front is where you urinate from, in the middle is the vagina opening and at the back is the anus where you defecate from. The front hole leads to the urethral opening, the second leads to the tube leading to the reproductive organs. The clitoris is at the front. The outer lips (labia), the clitoris and the vaginal opening are together known as the vulva. Simple and easy!

<u>Menstruation</u>

The most obvious sign of puberty is blood coming out through the vagina called menstruation. O.M.G!!!

The first time any young girl experiences menstruation is pretty scary. Questions, amazement and fear, are the mixed emotions that follow.

Where is the blood coming from?

Am I hurt?

Will I bleed to death?

Am I dying?

Do I have a wound somewhere inside me?

In its scientific terms, it is called "Menarche" and is a frightening thing for most girls because of the poorly informed older women, aunties, mothers and grandmothers. Once you tell them your new experience, they hold you by the hands, and lead you somewhere very private where no one else can hear you and as you are being led away, you are totally convinced you have done something wrong. Panic sets in!

These elderly women tell you to avoid all contacts with boys. Boys become a plague! Suddenly, you are expected to change your entire lifestyle without knowing why, except for this show of blood. This can create mixed feelings in a young girl's mind. You are quite sure this must be the end of your life.

I remember being fed such stories including amazing tales of pregnancy occurring without sex! For example, I was told never to let any boy cross over my legs if I was seated on the floor, as the immediate result would be a pregnancy. A whole new radical meaning of the Immaculate Conception! On a humorous note, I wonder why it is called "men-struation" but that is another subject!

PMS (Pre-Menstrual Syndrome) is a term used to describe the physical and emotional symptoms you may experience before menstruation. For instance, the breasts may feel sore, or become larger, and a breakout of spots (pimples) on the face may occur. You may feel tired and find it hard to concentrate. You get food cravings, or become very emotional. This is the period when everyone and everything irritates you-You know, the days when you feel mom, dad and the rest of the world just don't get it? And to imagine that some women experience P.M.S throughout their reproductive life cycle and they have to learn how to manage and deal with it.

During menstruation, some young girls refrain from various sorts of activities because of psychological strain, discomfort, headaches, cramps or the fear of getting "a stain" on their clothes.

You will eventually learn how to gauge your flow and know which size and absorbency type to buy and use.

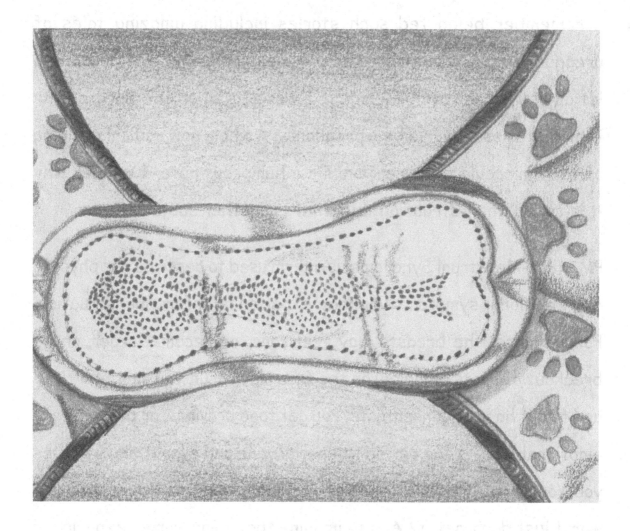

In ancient days, women washed, used and re-used rags specially kept for this purpose much as they used cloth napkins for babies. It was not the most hygienic method because of the possibility of infections. The sanitary towel, even though it has some discomfort, is a very safe way to go. It should be changed frequently at least every 3- 4 hours, regardless of the amount of flow. Used sanitary towels and tampons should be wrapped up and discarded in the trash. In most public restrooms there is a special repository or bin in each restroom where used sanitary towels and tampons can be disposed of. Always ensure that pads or tampons are disposed of appropriately.

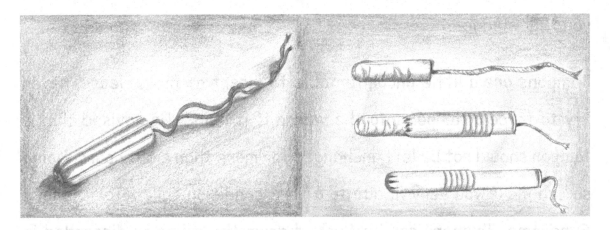

Non-applicator tampon   Tampon with applicator

What is the tampon? A tampon is like a small rolled up piece of cotton wool with a string at one end. You push a tampon into the vagina leaving the string hanging outside the body. The string is then used to pull the tampon after use. Some tampons come with applicators that help you properly insert the tampon. Since the tampon is inserted *into* the vagina, it usually stays there, and acts like a wine bottle cork. It holds and soaks in the blood flow. The advantage of the tampon is that it poses no problems when engaged in everyday activities or even swimming unlike the sanitary towel that can shift.

I do not suggest tampon use by young inexperienced girls. This is because the tampon could break the hymen which is in the vagina. What is this hymen? It is a small piece of thin skin that partly covers the vaginal opening. Sometimes the hymen breaks and bleeds slightly when a girl has sex for the first time, and sometimes there is no bleeding at all. Active sporting life can even break the hymen without your knowledge.

Tampons are a little uncomfortable to insert at first. Please, never try to force a tampon into the vagina if it hurts. Be advised that a tampon should not be left unchanged for more than eight hours. Doing so can make you very ill due to a rare condition called Toxic Shock Syndrome. Tampons can be flushed down the toilet or discarded in the same way as the sanitary towels.

Strict sanitary conditions must be adhered to during periods. It is a good idea to take a bath twice a day, particularly if you live in the tropics where it is humid and you sweat a lot.

Periods occur monthly (about every 28 days)

Some girls feel cramp-like pains during their periods. For some it could be an intense pain that requires medication. For others, exercising may help, cradling a hot water bottle may also help and yet for some girls, it may be more of a psychological unease that is induced by hormones. Being busy can take your mind off too.

Please note: If your period does not start when you expect it, and you have had sex, you could be pregnant. You must talk to an adult or see a doctor as soon as possible. It is important to do this even if you used some form of prevention as no contraceptive is guaranteed to be 100 % effective.

If you have not had sexual intercourse and your period doesn't come when you expect it to, there is probably no need to worry. There are many things that can cause changes to your periods for example being unwell, changing your diet, doing excessive amounts of exercise or feeling stressed. Sometimes, the worry caused by a late period can delay it even further. If your period is delayed for several months, speaking to a doctor could help to identify the underlying cause.

In some communities, the onset of menstruation signals the entry into womanhood and is celebrated with much pomp and pageantry in ceremonies called "rites of passage". The girl is celebrated with feasting and dancing because she is now officially a woman.

The importance of virginity is also seen among certain tribes or cultures. After the wedding, the bridal party waits for the groom to bring out the blood-stained sheet that confirms the girl's virginity prior to marriage. An unstained sheet brought dishonor, shame and disgrace to the bride's parents. There have been stories of parents who have a blood mix portion ready to stain the sheets.

The rites of womanhood is not to be confused or taken to be the circumcision or female mutilation rites of passage which I know obtains in some cultures. As far as female circumcision is concerned, I do not subscribe to it because of the many dangers inherent with the practice and obviously, the lack of benefit to the woman. Many young girls have been stitched up in archaic manners of surgery without any form of concern or consideration. Female mutilation has been identified as one of the leading causes of sterility, frigidity and even death in women. The young girls who have suffered this horrendous ordeal of stitching have had difficulties with childbirth. It should be legally banned with serious punitive repercussions on those who continue the practice to protect the lives of the young girls who are subject to it.

Contraceptives for teenagers

Contraceptives mean you intentionally prevent the occurrence of pregnancy. When teenage girls talk, they naturally gravitate towards conversations about boys and sex. It becomes the "in-thing" and girls who are not "doing it" become outcasts. Here is a word of caution: don't ever feel pressured into having sex just because others are doing it. Contraceptives prevent fertilization in different ways.

- Barrier methods - which physically prevents sperm from swimming into the uterus and fertilizing the woman's egg.
- Hormonal methods - which alter a woman's hormonal cycle to prevent fertilization.
- For many people, barrier methods of contraceptives are best, because they not only prevent pregnancy, but also prevent HIV and other STD transmission.

Barrier methods of contraception include: the male condom, the female condom, and spermicidal foams or gels.

The male condom

The condom is made of rubber and fits on the penis like a hand glove. It stops the sperm from entering inside the girl's body. Condoms are not 100% safe and can rip or tear during sex.

Reflections

I remember the first time I saw a condom was when I picked it up from my cousin's room. I thought it was a balloon. I started blowing air into it. My cousin and his friends quickly snatched it and warned me sternly, not to play with "grown up" stuff. "What was the big fuss about?" I wondered.

Preteen Years (9-13)

The female condom

The female condom is not as popular as the male condom. It is bigger and worn inside the vagina much like using a tampon.

The diaphragm. The Diaphragm is made of rubber or silicone with a very flexible rim and a dome that has to be filled with spermicides before being folded and inserted in the vagina. It has to be inside the vagina for at least six hours before sex but not for more than twenty-four hours.

Spermicidal Methods

Spermicides are chemical agents that stop sperm from traveling up into the cervix. They come in different forms including creams, foaming tablets, gels and foam (which are squirted into the vagina using an applicator). They are not very effective against pregnancy when used on their own, but are quite effective when combined with a male condom. They are inserted shortly before intercourse. The spermicides can be messy.

Hormonal methods of contraception

These come in various forms of pills or injections. What does 'going on the pill' mean?

*It is a contraceptive in pill form which is taken orally (swallowed). How does it work?

It works on the hormones in women by "deceiving" the body into stopping ovulation, i.e. the release of an egg every month. The disadvantage of the pill is that it destabilizes the body's chemical balance. Reaction ranges from nausea, breast tenderness, bloating, heaviness, irritability, etc. It is also imperative not to forget to take these pills otherwise, protection against pregnancy is lost. The Progestogen-only pill has to be taken at the same time every day.

The Injection.

Depo-Provera is perhaps the most popular example of this type of contraceptive. An injection is administered once every twelve weeks. It is popular because it is easy to use.

The Contraceptive Implant: Example "implanol" is a small patch, a little over an inch long, which is inserted under the skin on the inside of a girl's arm. Instead of having to remember to take it every day, hormones are steadily released into a girl's body from the implant.

There is also "the morning after pill" – an emergency contraceptive that prevents pregnancy when taken after sex- it can work up to 72 hours after sex. It is most effective when taken within 24 hours of sex, and the sooner you take it, the better. It is not an effective way to avoid pregnancy and can have side effects.

The intrauterine device (IUD) and intrauterine system (IUS)

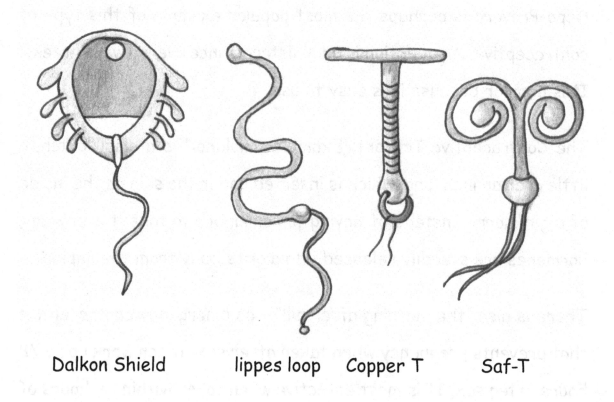

Dalkon Shield   lippes loop   Copper T   Saf-T

They are known as "the coil": they are very popularly used but are quite uncomfortable, cause severe harm and not generally considered safe for young girls who have had no children. The coil, like the copper T, is securely hooked unto the neck of the cervix and releases chemicals to kill the sperm. It is fixed and left with a thread or loop attached to it, dangling down.

This device is administered by a doctor under local anaesthesia and has specific renewal periods. It does not offer 100% protection against pregnancy and many babies have been conceived and born by women using the IUD.

Another example of the IUD is the Mirena IUC which is an estrogen-free intrauterine contraceptive device.

Sexually Transmitted Diseases (S.T.D)

In the process of writing this book and talking with teenagers, a recurring message I get is that a high percentage of teens are not taking precautions when having sex. They do not understand the gravity of the risk involved. They are adventurous and have the basic misunderstanding that terrible things happen to the "other girl not I."

For every young girl reading this, please note: Life is fun, but there are rules and regulations. If you break the rules, you have to pay the price!

To reiterate, abstinence is the best way to live at this stage because of the numerous benefits: spiritual, physical and psychological. There is so much time for everything. You need to concentrate on what is most important right now which is your education, financial independence and stability, preparing for life as a mentor and resource to others and having good clean fun! There will be so much time for sex in the future, in marriage and in life!

What are S.T.D's?

Sexually Transmitted Disease (STD) is an infection that can be caught by having sexual contact without protection with someone who is infected. Unfortunately, the only full protection from getting STDs is 100% abstinence. STDs are dangerous because many remain potentially latent yet cause severe damages on the lives of young girls or boys if left untreated.

Human Papilloma-Virus (hpv).

- Extremely lethal viral infection that leads to cervical cancer in women, and both anal and penile cancers in men.
- Undetected in most cases.
- Visible symptoms are warts or growth around the genital organs.
- The sad thing is you don't contact HPV from just sexual contact. Kissing infected areas or simply touching the infected area can lead to it.
- HPV is not curable, but it is manageable. You may treat genitals warts and changes to the cervix, but the virus remains.
- Girls should be given the HPV vaccine by the age of 11 or 12.

Chlamydia

One of the leading causes of pelvic inflammatory disease and/or sterility (inability to have children) in women.

- Destructive to the fallopian tubes.
- There may be no symptom.
- Detected by vaginal bleeding or burning when urinating.
- Infection by vaginal or anal sex.
- Treatment by prescription antibiotics.
- Very similar to gonorrhea.
- Associated with incidence of premature births, eye damage in infants
- Found in the cervix, urethra, the throat or rectum.

Gonorrhea:

The most common STD.

- Spreads by vaginal, oral or anal sex.
- Survives only in moist regions within the body and is found in the vagina, cervix, urethra, bladder, back of the throat and rectum.
- Can cause sterility.

- Symptoms include burning during urination, yellow vaginal discharge, fever, abdominal pain, nausea, backache, or pain during intercourse.
- Prevention is by barrier methods like using condoms.

Herpes

Genital herpes has no cure.

- Spread commonly by vaginal, oral, or anal sex and by touching the blisters that presents as one of the symptoms.
- Blisters that look like the common sore that somehow lasts long could be herpes.
- Virus travels to the nerve roots near the spinal cord.
- Symptoms include vaginal discharge; burning sensations, fever, muscle aches, or headaches.

Syphilis

Syphilis has 3 stages of development.

- Produces a painless ulcer known as a "chancre."
- The infection can be transmitted from contact with the ulcer. If the ulcer is in the mouth, merely kissing the infected individual can spread the infection.
- Secondary syphilis: is the systemic stage of the disease.

- Involves various organ systems of the body like the skin typically appearing on the palms of the hands or the bottoms of the feet. The skin rash is highly contagious.

- Syphilis symptoms can include fever, headaches, sore throat, hair loss white patches in the nose, mouth, and vagina.

- Tertiary syphilis is also systemic.

- Causes a variety of problems throughout the body including abnormal bulging of the large vessel leaving the heart, which results in heart problems, infection of the brain leading to a stroke, mental confusion, meningitis or brain infection, sight deterioration and deafness.

- All of these conditions are severe and often fatal.

- Women infected during pregnancy can pass it on to the fetus via the placenta and if untreated can lead to blindness of the infant or death.

- The penicillin antibiotic is used to treat syphilis.

Trichomoniasis (Trich)

Infects thousands of teenagers a year.

- Spread by vaginal sex.

- A parasitic infection that weakens the immune system, making a person more susceptible to HIV.

- Symptoms are heavy greenish vaginal discharge; genital itching or burning, abdominal pain; and frequent urination.
- Some experience no symptoms.

Hepatitis B

Hepatitis B causes inflammation of the liver.

- 30% cases worldwide, attributed to sexual transmission.
- Chronic form of Hepatitis B is dangerous to women and causes cirrhosis and cancer of the liver.
- Kissing and unprotected intercourse are methods of spreading this virus.
- Pregnant women can transmit it to the fetus.
- Symptoms appear in about 50% of cases and include jaundice, fever, nausea, swelling of the legs, fluid accumulation in the abdomen.
- A vaccine can prevent this virus.

Candida

A common yeast infection complaint by women sexually active or otherwise.

- Not an STD
- Affects women who frequently use antibiotics, taking oral or other types of contraceptives.

- Signs include white, cheese-like vaginal discharge.

- Sometimes there is swelling around the vaginal that itches or burns.

- Occurrence in the mouth is oral candidiasis or thrush common in infants and babies. The sign is thick white patches which may look like milk curds but usually can't be wiped away and can manifest as other skin infections.

- Can be treated with over-the-counter topical antifungal creams.

- Prevented by wearing clean cotton underwear, avoiding tight or synthetic- like nylon underwear that cause irritation, and wiping thoroughly after bathing or urinating. Avoid scented tampons.

Most common over-the-counter cure for yeast infection includes Monistat and other anti-fungal prescriptions.

- Test with home screening kit like Vagicil to be sure it is a yeast infection.

Ectoparasitic Infections

Ecto-parasites are transmitted by close physical contact, including sexual contact.

- Affect the skin or hair and cause itching.

- Examples are pubic lice and bugs, visible to the naked eye, that live on pubic hair and are most often associated with itching.

- Treatment is usually with 1% cream rinse of Permethrin or any shampoo with Lindane.

- Bedding and clothing must be washed with hot water

- All sexual partners must be treated for pubic lice and evaluated for other STDs. Other types of bugs that can be sexually transmitted include scabies.

Reflections

On an episode of "House" which is a series run on Fox Television Network in the USA, I watched with dismay, intrigue and fascination as a young girl contracted a bug infection by having unprotected sex. When nothing else seemed to work, I observed in total awe as Dr. Gregory House vaginally probed and searched her fragile genitals and cervix to bring out the still-living six-legged parasite! It was a mind-blowing episode for me.

Human Immunodeficiency Virus (HIV)

The human immunodeficiency virus (HIV) causes AIDS (acquired immunodeficiency syndrome).

- Deadly and incurable.

- Body's defenses against some illnesses are broken down.

- People with AIDS can get many different kinds of diseases like pneumonia, tuberculosis, e.t.c which a healthy person's body would normally fight off quite easily.

Reflection:

In 2006, we went on a mission visit to one of the villages in Nigeria, Africa. I used the opportunity of the visit to talk to different groups of young girls about teenage struggles and healthcare.

In one of these groups, I developed a relationship with a young girl called Rita. As time went on, Rita informed me that she had a friend(name and family name withheld for privacy and confidentiality) who was being kept away from people because she had been "cursed" and sent back from abroad with a terrible ailment. On her arrival from abroad, the sick girl arrived at her family house. Everyone ran away as if she was a ghost because of the news that had spread. Rita further informed me that there was a doctor who occasionally saw the girl and very intrigued, I asked to be taken to the doctor.

He informed me that the girl had AIDS, and the parents had quarantined her. They could not afford the medications and were afraid that they would be ostracized by the community.

I asked Rita to take us to the house, and together with the doctor, we drove until we got to the young girl's home.

The parents were in and as soon as we asked for the young girl, their welcoming countenance changed. They became hostile, defensive and withdrawn. I pleaded with them that we only wanted to assist.

After what seemed like eternity, the mother broke down in tears and begged the father to let us see her. He pointed to the back of the house, and like a man buckling under the gravity of the situation, sat down heavily and stared at the floor.

The back of the house was like a chicken shed or poultry. It was a mini-livestock habitat and the smell of cow dung filled the still air. It was suffocating. There was a make shift dilapidating shed with one little window and a very secured door. The door had massive chains and padlocks. The doctor pointed and said "she is there." I stood still as the goose bumps ran through me. Rita walked around the shed, calling out her name. There was shuffling of the feet and a pained response from inside.

A little face, no older than twenty peeped from the window. I looked at the face: so sweet, so innocent looking, so lined up with pain, so old beyond its years. My heart was broken. What had this young girl done to deserve this treatment?

She suddenly snarled from the window and made furtive desperate launches at the door. Obviously, survival instincts had taught her to be aggressive and defensive. Her hair had been shaved off from what I could see and she was emaciated. I asked for the door to be open and Rita said this was impossible. I turned to go back, only to bump into the mother who calmly said her daughter was not to have any physical contact with anyone. She had not been given a bath for a long time, was contained by the use of a stick and was being fed through the window. Why? I asked. Well, the mother explained, the girl had to be kept away from people because she had brought shame to the family. She had been taken out of the country by her sister-in-law who resided in Italy at age sixteen and only did as her aunt instructed, but ended up in this way. The aunt sent her back when she kept falling ill. I understood.

I explained that this girl could live a normal life if only she could get some help. I assured her we could help her in terms of medication but that their treatment of this poor girl was undeserved. This was a fate worse than death for her. "Please, please", called a weak voice from the shed. Our appeals fell on deaf ears and we left. That night, I tossed and turned, unable to sleep, very tortured by the pained haunted look in the girl's eyes.

We secured some medication for the girl and went back to the home. This time, the door was opened and we brought the girl out. She was frail and could barely stand up. I assisted her to sit with me. She reached out and touched my hand. Then she smiled. She was a beautiful shadow with an angelic smile. She spoke slowly and painfully that she had missed the human touch and now felt human again. She smelled so badly; weeks of not been cleaned up. Her sores were festering and flies were buzzing all around her. She coughed and spat. Then she asked for water to drink and as Rita ran to get some, she laid her head on my lap. I asked for hot water to wash her up. The water took some time to boil and it was an uncomfortable silence since the parents stood stoically beside us. As I caressed her head, I looked up to talk to them and reassured them that their daughter would be ok.

Suddenly, the doctor signaled to me. I did not understand until he pointed at the girl cradled on my leg. She had a smile on her face and her eyes stared lifelessly ahead. She was still. Silent. Dead.

There are so many cases like this young girl's story. AIDS is ravaging the world at such an alarming rate, yet the unhealthy practices that causes this disease goes on, unabated.

AIDS is not contracted through prostitution or sex alone. Using or sharing a needle of an infected person, tainted blood transfusions and mother to child transmission during pregnancy are at-risk behaviors. HIV is present in blood, semen, vaginal secretions, breast milk, saliva, tears, sweat, and urine. Interestingly, tattoos and body piercing are accounting for a growing number of HIV cases in teens today. In my book *"Tangled"*, the young heroine, Onyinye, contracts AIDS through the needle used for her hair weave! She was also circumcised using razor blades that may not have been sterilized.

Quite a lot of teenagers sew weaves for each other on campus. Please use your own needles. If you do manicure or pedicure, pierce body parts or shape your eyebrows, please be careful. If you go to a guys' house, don't just go using his shaving stick!

Symptoms of AIDS include rapid weight loss, prolonged fever, frequent diarrhea and extreme fatigue. There are many infected people without any symptoms and this is because incubation period of the disease takes a long time, up to several years before a person develops full blown AIDS.

That very fine young man you want to date may have HIV AIDS!

A recent disturbing trend is among business men or travelers who go back and forth continents and engage in reckless and careless sexual escapades with young girls and who do not care to ask for protection.

Many have confessed to illicit affairs and said they never used a condom. They return home and put their partners at risk.

AIDS is an epidemic brewing: a keg of gunpowder, a smoldering volcano, a hurricane of tremendous proportion and when it hits... So many lives would be lost!!!

There are women and men who are aware of the non-monogamous relationships that they are in, yet do nothing or are too scared to insist on a condom.

However, please, people with AIDS should not be treated like the plague! They should not be ostracized, maligned or discriminated against. You can live with them, they can get married, have children: if they know how to deal with the situation.

Although AIDS gets far less media attention than it did in decades past, an estimated 42 million people worldwide are still living with AIDS or HIV (human immunodeficiency virus, which causes AIDS), with more than 3 million dying every year from AIDS-related illnesses

Finally, if you think you have an STD, go to a doctor or a clinic right away. Additionally, abstain from further sexual activity to avoid infecting your partner(s). It is recommended that your partners get tested. Untreated STDs can be dangerous - if you don't get help, you may not be able to have children later in life, or it can increase your risk of cervical cancer.

Many young girls are scared of reporting STDs to their parents and to professionals. Well, it is better to face the anger of parents for a short while, than to lose your chance of procreating or facing death. Most (but not all) clinics have a confidentiality policy, and will respect the patient's right to privacy. Some places will want you to bring parental consent.

A test could be a simple urine or blood sample, or a swab from the vagina or penis. If you think that you may already have passed on the infection to someone else, tell him, so that he may get tested too. If the clinic gives you antibiotics or medication, make sure that you follow the instructions and complete the course of treatment - otherwise the STD may recur.

STDs can be prevented, but the risks are so downplayed that most people have lost their fear of contracting STDs.

Douching: Is a way of cleaning out the vagina by forcing or squirting medically prepared solutions into it to flush discharge. They are said to treat certain STD's or conditions and are available over the counter. A school of researchers argue that douching is not necessary and can even create more problems in the vagina cavity.

Pregnancy

Teenage pregnancy is usually the worst fear of a teenage girl's parents because of the predictably grave consequences.

- Girl is not physically developed enough for childbearing.

- Usually causes disruption in academic or future pursuits.

- First pregnancies are usually a mistake.

- Young girls believe pregnancy occurs only after it happens more than once. What a fib! Please make no mistakes. Pregnancy can, and does occur the first time you have sex if you do not take precaution during sexual intercourse.

How does pregnancy occur?

Girls' reproduction organs *(inside)*

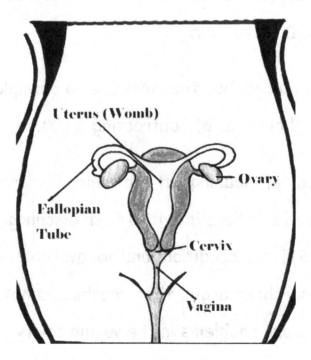

- Two small organs called the ovaries contain hundreds of tiny sex cells called "eggs".
- At puberty, they get released monthly in a process called ovulation. Between 11 and 14 days after the egg is released, it waits for semen and when there is none, it disintegrates, flows out, and the process repeats itself in a cyclical form called the menstrual cycle.
- Between these 11 to 14 days, fertility is highly possible.
- Practitioners of the "Billings" method of abstinence avoid this period (Billings is encouraged and practiced by Catholics)
- Pregnancy can occur anytime during a circle. There is no 100% safe method of contraceptives. Period.

If sex and ejaculation occurs, what happens?

- Millions of sperms set for the journey to find the egg.
- They swim through the uterine walls into the fallopian tubes.
- The egg is released by the ovary and makes its way into the uterus via the fallopian tubes.
- Out of the millions of tiny sperms, only one can penetrate the egg.
- Once this happens, fertilization has occurred.
- The fertilized egg divides into more cells and becomes a ball or zygote and continues through the tubes to the uterine

walls about 3-4 days after fertilization. This ball or zygote then attaches to the lining of the uterus and it is at this point that we say a girl is pregnant.

- You could still "spot" (blood-stained underpants) and be pregnant!

Please note:

1. The fact that eggs are released at certain times of the month does not mean you cannot get pregnant during other times. In other words, no date or time is safe. Ovulation days vary from girl to girl.

2. Sperm survive for up to 72 hours after release and can 'hang around' waiting for an egg to be released.

3. You must use a form of birth control or contraceptive any time you have sex to prevent pregnancy and STDs.

4. You can get pregnant the first time you have unprotected sex!

5. Like said earlier, due to the inconsistency and predictability of ovulation, you can still get pregnant during your period.

6. Withdrawal method is no method. The pre-come, that is the liquid that comes before the ejaculation, sometimes contains sperms.

7. You can have sex standing, sitting, upside down, in whatever position you think will drain the sperm or prevent it from going into the womb. It does not work. Sperms swim in all directions.

*If pregnancy is confirmed by testing, the usual option for a young unprepared girl is either have the baby, have it and give out for adoption or go through the dreaded abortion.

ABORTIONS

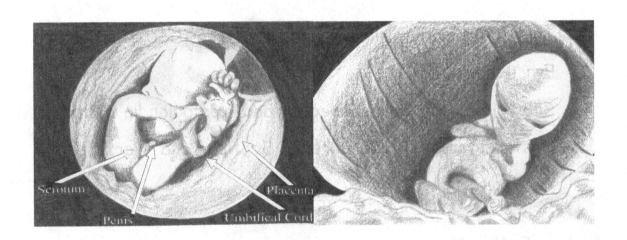

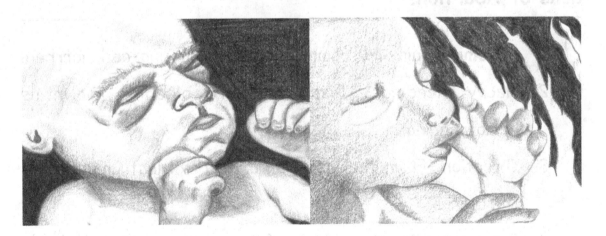

The online dictionary defines abortion in 3 ways:

1. Any of various surgical methods for terminating a pregnancy, esp. during the first six months.

2. <u>Voluntary abortion.</u> The removal of an embryo or fetus from the uterus in order to end a pregnancy.

3. Also called <u>spontaneous abortion.</u> MISCARRIAGE

There are 3 main methods of abortion that depend largely upon the stage of pregnancy and the size of the unborn child.

1. Suction abortions: Dilation and Curettage (D&C, Dilation and Evacuation (D&E).

2. Salt Poisoning or Saline Injection and Prostaglandin Chemical.

3. Hysterectomy or Caesarean Section and Partial-Birth Abortion.

Risks of Abortion.

1. Abdominal pain and cramping, nausea, vomiting, and diarrhea.

2. Heavy Bleeding - Risk of severe bleeding known as hemorrhaging.

3. Infection –From the insertion of medical instruments into the uterus

4. Incomplete Abortion - Some fetal parts may be mistakenly left inside after the abortion. Bleeding and infection may result.

5. Sepsis – A number of RU486 or mifepristone users have died as a result of sepsis (total body infection).

6. Anesthesia – Complications may result in convulsions, heart attack, and in some cases, death.

7. Damage to the Cervix - The cervix may be cut, torn, or damaged by abortion instruments.

8. Scarring of the Uterine Lining – Suction tubing, curettes, and other abortion instruments may cause permanent scarring of the uterine lining.

9. Perforation of the Uterus - The uterus may be punctured or torn by abortion instruments. Major surgery may be required, including removal of the uterus (known as a hysterectomy).

10. Damage to Internal Organs - When the uterus is punctured or torn, there is also a risk that damage will occur to nearby organs such as the bowel and bladder.

11. Women who undergo one or more induced abortions carry a significantly increased risk of delivering prematurely in the future.

12. Death from all these complications.

Appearance and Hygiene Basics.

Reflection

"Go back to your room and change to something decent!"

Have you heard parents yell this phrase over and over? I have seen parents totally freak out when their teenage daughters come out from their rooms dressed for school. The parents look in amazement at the fashion style of the teenage girls: the spaghetti tops, net-see-through blouses, short mini-skirts, frizzled, spiked or gel-up hair, painted toe-nails in multiple colors and they shake their heads and sigh. "What is this world turning to?" they often ponder.

Children on the other hand consider their parents old-fashioned and ancient! The striped shirts, suspenders, bow-ties, and tuxedos in fact, anything parents are wearing is considered so old and definitely not trendy.

Fashion is a generational issue. Trends change, revolve, fade and then get back in vogue.

What parents seek most is that their teenage daughters are appropriately and decently attired. They do not want them running around 'naked" or like young boys do these days, "sagging" Parents want cleanliness and like my teachers used to say, "Cleanliness is next to Godliness".

We will start with head hair.

African or Black: Kinky or curly hair as seen on people of African descent must be combed thoroughly or it becomes "nappy" and tangled up like dreadlocks or twists. Black hair is versatile. It can be woven, matted, texturized (softened chemically). If you must use a texturizer, use one that has no lye in it, particularly if dealing with tender scalp. Lye contains agents that can burn the scalp.

For young girls, a good warm hair blower and a comb, gently running from roots to tip can soften the kinky black hair and make it manageable enough to braid. Don't forget to use your hand to hold down the hair at the roots before combing through so you are not pulling and tugging at the scalp causing pain.

I don't believe young children need to have hair-extensions in their hair because it pulls the hair from the roots particularly from the crown and nape, so that you find children going "bald" very early.

And if you must, don't let it be braided too tight. A good hair cream should be applied to the scalp.

White or Caucasian: Hair should be washed and shampooed every week too. It is a little more challenging to braid because of the silky texture, but with a little creativity, it is possible. For those who are bi-racial, they can braid their hair or wear it straight. Curlers are used in hair of all types to add waves or curls into it. Pink oil softens hair while hair styling sprays and mousse make it stiff and gives perceived volume. The sebaceous glands secrete oils that may cause hair follicles to clog up because oil combines with dirt and blocks off the hair pores. Hair needs to be washed frequently to keep oils and dirt from clogging up the pores and causing dandruffs.

Not keeping the hair groomed can cause hair and head problems like head lice and ringworm.

Head lice

Like pubic hair lice, head lice are a transferable problem and are actually very common.

- Found on the head, scalp, behind the ears and near the neckline at the back of the neck.
- Head lice hold on to hair with hook-like claws that are found at the end of each of their six legs.
- The signs and symptoms are: a tickling feeling of something moving in the hair, itching (caused by the allergic reaction to the bites); sores on the head (caused by scratching); and irritability.

Reflection

Growing up, we frequently contracted head lice because we shared combs, slept on each other's beds and pillows or exchanged berets and scarves. Please do not share combs! If you must, do sterilize them first. To combat the lice, we used all sorts of sprays including ant, mosquitoes, bugs, roach spray on our heads and would cover tight with a shower cap secured by a head scarf.

Elimination is by thorough fumigation and cleaning of the home.

Ring worm

- Two types: the scalp and the skin ringworm.
- Scalp ringworm is common among children and is caused by a fungal infection. It causes a red, crusty, scaly patch often shaped like a ring. Up to 50% of hair loss among children is caused by scalp ringworm.
- Scalp ringworm must be treated systemically (with medicine that spreads throughout the body) to penetrate the hair follicle.
- Griseofulvin, Fulvicin and Grisactin have been the drug of choice since 1958 because of its safety. The usual dose involves taking the medicine every day. Therapy should

continue until the culture shows that no fungi are present. Other types of medication include Itraconazole (Sporanox) fluconazole (Diflucan) terbinafine (Lamisil)

- Another hair problem is dandruff or psoriasis. It is the flaky white powdery substance that is seen on the scalp. It can be controlled by shampoo containing sulphur as an active ingredient e.g. selsun blue.

Disturbing Body Hair

Reflection

Some girls get more than a fair share of body hair! So you start wondering...ok, why won't this hair grow on my head, rather than on my legs, face, hands etc...what's up with that? In my teenage years, we cruelly referred to very hairy girls as "Homo Sapiens or Homo Erectus". If you remember your history, the hairy early man was called "Homo Erectus" There was a neighbor of ours when I was growing up and she has a full chin of beard! Her husband was a puny man, and we made fun of them: calling her the "he-goat husband". We would clap and jeer at her as she made her way home every evening. Unfortunately, they had no children and of course, the neighborhood wasted no time in declaring her a "witch". It was all fun for us, but it must have been agonizing for her. We were so mean!

Facial Hair:

- Do not pluck out facial hairs. Why? They multiply! As you take one out, twenty would pop out. Blame it on those hormones that you have absolutely no control over!

- You can get rid of unwanted hair permanently by electrolysis or other modern scientific methods.

- Creams or blades would only aggravate the skin, especially if not done properly. They may take off the surface hair but leave the roots intact.

- Hair under both arms and on the surface/body of the vagina is another feature of puberty.

- Some girls may decide to leave the hair on their legs and under their arms as is or shave it. It's all up to you and what you are comfortable with.

- You can use a traditional razor with a shaving cream or gel or you can use an electric razor.

- If you use a regular razor, make sure the blade is new and sharp to prevent cuts and nicks.

- Shaving cream and gel are often better than soap because they make it easier to pull the razor against your skin.

- Some of the newer razors contain shaving gel right in the blade area, making even beginners feel comfortable shaving.

Hands and Feet: Finger Nails and Toes.

- Finger nails are an extension of the skin.

- Keep them clean and well cut to prevent germs.

- Wash hands every time you use the bathroom will prevent spread of some diseases since your hands go to your mouth frequently.

- Use a hand sanitizer that kills 99% germs whenever possible.

- Beautifully groomed nails are attractive: they speak volumes of who you are. They may not grow hard or perfect, you can experiment with nail hardeners, or nail polish and false nails...but a note of caution: fixing false nail extensions CAN destroy the nail cuticle.

- Use moisturizers regularly particularly after being immersed in water. This will prevent your hands from becoming dry.

- The heels or soles get scaly when not constantly moisturized and needs to be exfoliated regularly.

- You can mix a paste of lime, ginger, orange, sugar, salt, baking soda and oatmeal granules to scrub the dead skin off. Some people use a pumice stone.

- Wearing ill-fitting tight shoes, you create the thick dead skin called calluses. Please don't use a blade or scissors to try to get rid of calluses. You can get infected that way. Keep feet dry with cornstarch.

Skin Care

The skin is often the first thing people notice on you, particularly the face and so, not surprisingly, skin cream industry is a multibillion dollar one. Young girls fret about their skin appearance.

- Hormones will cause changes during puberty

- Like pimples, eczemas or acne.

- A warning...there is no permanent cure for some of these conditions. It is a temporary phase.

- Skin problem may go with age but some may be genetic and re-occur periodically.

- Do not to pick at, or squeeze pimples or spots because this can cause an infection.

- Wash your face more often with mild non- perfumed or antiseptic soap and warm water and more especially if you use make-up or sunscreen

- Do not scrub the face too.

- Common solutions

- Eczema is itchy and flaky. It can be managed with creams containing Cortaid or cortisones.

- Dryness of the skin could be a problem so it is imperative to moisturize the skin daily.

- If neglected, the skin, like every other organ, would break, bleed and get infected.

- You can use antiseptic soaps to help combat skin problems.

- Do not use products that contain harsh or skin bleaching agents because they destroy the skin's main function as a guard and protector of the body.

Skin Types

Everyone has a special type of skin, so what may work for one person may not work for another. Some people have very oily skins, others have dry skins and each skin type has its peculiar challenges.

Like those with oily skins, particularly on the face, they may develop a "T-Zone" which means more shine and oil secreted from the forehead down to the chin and across.(like yours truly!) There are paper blotters, oil-free powders, and other products to combat oil on the face. However, this is a surface remedy because the oil-secreting glands are skin-deep. Oils from your hair can also cause spots, so keeping your hair clean and out of your face does help.

Some people find that eating less fatty foods (such as chips and chocolate) and drinking lots of water can help. Water is the one thing that you cannot over indulge in. God-given water is the best detoxification for the body and it is recommended that you drink eight 8 ounces of water daily. Water keeps us hydrated, maintain homeostasis, and cleanses the body by flushing out impurities. You should stay away from sugary drinks as well.

Reflection

As a teenager, I had, and still periodically, have pimples. I tried toothpaste, baking soda, neomedrol, benzyoxide, topgel, sand: to name a few. They made my skin burn, and break. Sometimes, I would look like a fried lobster because of the scaling and peeling skin. Yet, they never solved the problem.

Some people have tried Proactive and other modern acne remedies. To get rid of spots, I tried the Shirley, Island, e.t.c. They may work if you can dab on the spots only but for most people, they end up giving an uneven facial tone and your face becomes lighter than your body!

I personally, have come to respect the fact that the skin and body does heal itself. And there are some things that do not in any way take away from who you are. You need to accept your make up.

The urge to become lighter or brighter by using bleaching creams comes as a result of low self esteem and the media's portrayal of light-skinned women. The movie actresses that the media claims are most popular are usually the light-skinned ones. Thankfully, there are more strong portrayals these days of women and people of very dark colors. The result of using bleaching agents is simple: skin cancers, skin diseases and discoloration of the skin.

Please accept your uniqueness and be proud of who you are.

Bad Breath

Bad breath is medically called halitosis. It can result from either poor dental health habits and is made worse by the types of foods you eat.

Nothing defeats good morale like bad breath. Imagine people putting their hands up to cover their nose when you are talking! Bad breath can be controlled or checked. There are various myths about bad breath. Please don't breathe into your hands, sniffing, and thinking "I will know." There is a big difference in breathing or blowing air into your hands and carrying out a conversation. A comedian I know once said "if you win arguments all the time, know you must have bad breath!"

- During the food absorption process, food travels into the stomach, then into the blood stream.
- It is also taken into the lungs and given off in your breath.
- If you eat foods with strong odors like garlic or onions, brushing, flossing or mouthwash will cover up the odor

temporarily. The odor will not go away completely until the foods have passed through your body.

- Other causes of bad breath include bacteria in the mouth and stomach.

- Intestinal disturbances, bowel sluggishness, sinus or throat infections, tobacco or alcohol use, milk intolerance, not drinking enough water and keeping the body hydrated, dental problems like gaps, crooked teeth, festering tooth decays, vitamin deficiencies, especially vitamin C and niacin, and chewing gum or eating candy because the sugar can leave a residue that promotes rapid bacterial growth.

- Use a good toothbrush and change it every 1-2 months.

- The method of brushing also counts. Brush up, down, inside, then up and down, the premolars, molars, incisors, and behind the tongue area. *Note that brushing your teeth alone will not take care of bad breath. Try to brush for at least 1 minute.

- Use a good toothpaste that has Sodium fluoride with tartar protection that either help to whiten the teeth or prevent cavities.

- Mouth rinses with antiseptic ingredients that kill the germs that cause bad breath and plaque are essential.

- Flossing helps get rid of the plaques that hide and stick between the teeth.

- If you follow these procedures strictly and still have bad breath, then you should consult a doctor immediately. You should visit the dentist at least twice a year whether or not you have a problem.
- You may need to wear braces to straighten crooked teeth.

Body Odor

Every person is born with a special and unique smell. It is not usually unpleasant.

- Bad Body Odor is the unpleasant smell that is emitted by the body when bacteria come in contact with sweat.
- The most common body parts that are associated with body odor include hair, feet, groin, skin, underarms (armpits), genitals, pubic hair, belly button and ears.
- With puberty, glands not only become more active, they also begin to secrete different stronger smelling chemicals into the sweat.
- The best way to keep the body clean is to bath or shower every day using a mild soap and warm water. In tropical and humid regions, this is essential. Take note of areas of the body that has crevices or folds or secretions.

- Wearing fresh clean cotton clothes, socks, and underwear each day can also help you stay and feel clean.

- Deodorants get rid of the odor of sweat by covering it up, and antiperspirants actually stop or dry up perspiration. They come in sticks, roll-ons, gels, sprays, and creams.

- Sprinkle some baking soda, talc, baby powder or cornstarch under the arms.

- Wash clothes with an odor-fighting detergent. If necessary, take a change of clothes or underwear with you to school.

- Drink eight 8-ounce glasses of water to cleanse the system.

- Staying away from certain foods garlic that emits very highly pungent smells. The skin gland secretes or gets rid of these impurities through sweat that stays on the skin (except you take a shower)

- Exercising is a good way to get rid of waste products because you sweat it out and cool off.

- Vagina disease and discharge could also cause body odor. Normal vagina discharge does not have a bad odor.

Diet & Exercise

- Going without food is dangerous because the stomach produces acidic enzymes which act on the walls of the stomach and intestines producing ulcers.

- Breakfast is an important meal of the day.

- Snacking on healthy foods like fruits during the day.

- Too much of anything is bad, so moderation is key. Carbohydrates, fried food and red meat without workout can clog the arteries, produce high level of cholesterol and cause high blood pressure and cause obesity

- Cardio activity for at least 30 to 60 minutes a day builds muscles, boost metabolism and keep joints working well.

Etiquette

In movies with royal noble characters, we see the ladies exhibit prim and proper behaviors. The word "lady" connotes one with very graceful manners. You will recognize ladies by their poise, elegance and carriage. They stand out distinctly.

Here are some ground rules.

1. Absolutely no gum chewing.

2. There is a difference between being a girl and a boy. No "tom-boy" gestures or antics.

3. Ladies do not slur when talking.

4. They do not pick their nose.

5. Do not wear rough rumbled clothes.

6. Do not show underwear- amazing that in the name of "fashion" ladies show off their "thongs"

7. Ladies sit upright with feet crossed at the ankles and tucked under the chair.

8. Do not raise their voices, are not boisterous or loquacious. This is not the same thing as being assertive when necessary.

9. Use fresh panty liners daily.

Wipe toilet seats with clean tissue before sitting. If possible and available, use seat liners. Flush before and after use of toilet. Be very careful that you don't allow urine from inside the toilet splash up into you. Please wipe front to back to prevent diseases from passing from the anus to the vagina area. Finally, when you flush, do not use your bare hands. Use either your feet or use tissue paper to handle public toilet doors, faucets and dispensers.

10. Wash hands thoroughly, including inside the finger tips with soap and water for at least 2 minutes.

11. Use fresh underwear every day.

A lady's purse or handbag tells a lot about her. These are suggestions of things you might want to keep in your purse or handbag.

1. A perfumed hand lotion. You should carry in your purse a hand lotion that smells good

2. 1 lip gloss.

3. 1 sanitary towel (you never know!)

4. 1 panty liner.

5. Some Kleenex tissue or handkerchief.

6. 1 hair brush or comb.

7. Facial powder or blotting paper that takes off the shine off the face from oil secretions: Oily t-zones!

8. Condoms. As you grow older, I think you should keep a condom somewhere.

   Now, come on parents!! I don't want parents to start screaming or raising their eyebrows. While not promoting immorality there must be preventive measures taken. It is advisable to have a condom handy in your purse, even if society frowns. You need to protect yourself.

9. A deodorant stick and a small bottle of perfume or body spray.

10. A pack of mints or dental floss to freshen the breath periodically.

11. Also, a small mirror in your purse would be good so that after eating, you can check your teeth to see if you have food particles between them.

12. The occasional journal or diary.

13. A small travel-size hand sanitizer.

2.
~

PSYCHOLOGICAL

Now we shall deal with the psychological. Talk about major U.F.O invasion! It is a vast subject area that deals with peer pressure, anxiety, social isolation, memories, drugs, rape, sexual abuse, depression and suicide.

Early Childhood

From toddler stages, children start to retain some images or events that occur in their lives. They particularly remember some, but through growing up, events or memories get buried deep within the consciousness. It is what Sigmund Freud refers to as "the unconscious mind".

He likened events that we remember in our adulthood as a tip of the iceberg. Truly in life, we have flash backs or quick insights into things that occurred when we were very young. Our mind learns to have "selective retentions" but on occasions, those events, particularly if very traumatic or emotional, come out to play in adolescence or adulthood. If for example, a child is sexually molested at age 5, the people around may try to shield the child from it. They may not refer or talk about it. After a while, it seems it never happened. But there is already a psychological impact. Some children may exhibit it, some may not. But as the child grows, she will get flashbacks. If you had some traumatic events as a child, here are tips of what you need to do.

1. Talk about it. There is nothing new under the sun. Talking to someone you trust would be therapeutic and lighten the load.

2. Forgive any offenders. If offender is still alive and free, report to the authorities.

3. Learn from it. The German Philosopher Friedrich Nietzsche said "what does not kill me can only make me stronger".

4. Teach others. You never learn go through an experience to keep it to yourself. Someone else could benefit from your experience. Not talking about things leads to withdrawals, anger issues, depression and other psychological issues.

There are some interesting behavioral psychological patterns that young girls typically exhibit across cultures.

- **Anorexia**: when young girls starve themselves to death. They indulge in purging or abusing laxatives to retain the ideal body image of being slim or thin. After a while they critically fall sick.
- **Bulimia**: They always have the urge to eat, and then they go and force it all out. They develop ulcers in the throats and mouth.

These two are a result of an expected or ideal body image.

Reflection.

As a young very slim girl, mine was quite the opposite, but it was a sickness. I tried so hard to add on weight because I was so slim. I ate a lot, took a drink called "egovin" "ribena" to boost my appetite. It did not work.

At 16, I was invited to model where I found so many other young girls who were as slim. Interestingly, we were being asked the secret to our svelte look! That taught me a lesson: The grass always looks greener on the other side. We always seem to want what the other girl has.

- **Obesity:** On the opposite end of being thin, is being obese. Big-boned teenagers are always a target of taunts and name calling in school. Some of these girls end up staying away from others.

Reflection

As long as you are healthy, you eat and exercise right, and your doctor gives you a clean bill of health, believe in yourself. It could be your genetic structure. It is in our uniqueness that we are all made to look different and special. This is why I love women like Monique, Mandisa, Camrym Manheim Chaka Khan, Kathy Bates, Aretha Franklin, Kate Winslet and Oprah.

How boring it would have been if the world was full of the same colors, races, sizes and body structures!

- **Anti-Social:** These girls do not want to be around anybody. They have no interest in any activities, making friends, extra-curricular activities and keep their heads buried in books or activities that do not involve any form of interactions with others.

Reading is great, but being well-rounded is a better preparatory trait to adjusting in life. You should belong to a social club, learn to make friends. A common saying on campus is "Go through the school and let the school go through you". Think about this: the friends you make now form the network that will impact you most in life! So why not become more out-going, amiable, sociable and agreeable. In life, you can only move up with the right attitude!

A lot of anti-social behavioral issues come from the family environment. If there is sadness, insecurity or abuse, such girls are bound to be anti-social. Girls graduate from this stage into depression.

- **Depression:** is a serious problem for teens and affects girls more than boys. You become withdrawn, nothing seems interesting, you derive no joy in life, have no sense of self-worth, you simply want to crawl and stay alone, preferably in bed. At the height of depression comes obsessive indulgence in sex, food or alcohol.

  Quite a lot of young girls get this bug when they first get heartbroken by a young boy. Let me tell you, staying alone in self-pity does not help anybody least of all you! Particularly since the boy is probably blissfully unaware of what you are going through and is most likely chatting up another female right now! This is part of growing up and it may hit you again, and again in life as you learn that all relationships do not end as you think they should.

  People will disappoint you in life. You are not the first girl this is happening to, you are not the only one experiencing those emotions right now, and you certainly will not be the last. Your attitude in this should be of a growing sense of self-worth: you are more than this and of more value in life. You need to go on with life and learn from that experience. Channel that energy to something positively rewarding. Depression is a terrible thing and some people need medication to cope with it.

- **Suicide:** Depression sometimes leads into suicide. Rate of teenage suicides have been rising in recent times. The signs to watch for include hopelessness, isolation, abuse, excessive talking about it, obsession about death, the media and celebration of suicide cases, want for attention and ancestral patterns.

Reflection

I witnessed a suicide case while in college. It happened while we were taking a class on one cold morning in Jos. Our academic center was surrounded by a small "village" community of hostels where students who did not get regular accommodation in the student's hostels found some refuge. The university community had beautiful topography of undulating hilltops, breathtaking plateaus and gorgeous scenery and from the academic halls, we overlooked these village communities

This day, suddenly, piercing screams, accompanied by agonized wails resounded in the air. Our lecturer was immediately distracted by the noise and stepped outside to see what was going on. We exchanged puzzled looks as we saw people running and unable to stand the tension, we rushed out, leaving our alarmed lecturer standing by the door.

Right now, all we could see was the thick black smoke that had engulfed a portion of the village. People were going berserk, running around, getting buckets of water to douse and contain the fire that was threatening to spread. What could have happened? Did someone forget to turn off a stove? Was someone ironing a shirt when the lights went out?

No. We later found out that a young teenage student had set herself ablaze because she had been jilted by her boyfriend of two years. He had become involved with a freshman.

No matter how bad a situation is, there is always a solution, and suicide is not an answer.

One day, you would look back at your life and wonder how you got through certain situations. It could be dark, but only for a while.

Every painful moment is an opportunity to retool, re-learn, re-invent.

Abraham Lincoln tried to be president of the United States of America twice and failed. He did not give up. He tried again and became the 16th president. When he failed, he did not quit, he did not think that was the end. He tried again!

- **Snobs:** In school we had those who would look at us from beneath their noses. We did not have the same social influence or belong to the same social class. They were bossy, rude, arrogant, self-opinionated, self-centered , had a grandiose image of themselves and selfish. It's what psychologist would call a Narcissist personality. I did not realize they had a disorder. They were insecure.

  You must realize that this is a trait that even adults suffer from. They use their material possession to cover up their shallowness. Often times, they use their status to make friends and along the way, find out that these friends only associate with them for financial gains. Many suffer silently and are lonely. They look outwardly like happy, self-assured achievers but are inwardly very lonely.

- **Bullies.** These are different from the snobs. They are often from abusive homes and lack love. They pick on smaller girls and are the worst cowards. If you meet a bully, don't back down when they try to intimidate you. No matter how small you are, stand up and talk back, then walk away. There are girls like this in most schools. Internet bullying has become so popular now with advanced technology. Emails, text messages, social networks have created the opportunity of being able to access global information easily and many people have abused this. "People" Magazine of October 13th, 2010, shows the story of young children who have been victimized by internet bullying. It is not a funny thing. Globally, sometimes children can be cruel. Some do it out of mischief, ignorance, or just to be popular or get at you. There have been so many other cases of children committing suicide after cases of bullying. It can be hurtful and parents have a huge role to play in helping children understand from early childhood that all children are precious and equal not only in the eyes of God, but in their eyes as well.

It is easy to preach to children, but what do they see you practice or manifest? Do you discriminate or are you prejudiced as parents? Well, that is who your child would become. Children are usually blind to negative differences in each other until parents "teach" these subliminal messages. Parents that see nothing wrong in comments made by their little children such as

"I will not let you or your type come to my party?" should re-examine themselves quickly. Where on earth could a child hear or learn that from? All fingers point to parents who in their privacy exhibit these traits that their children in turn, learn and imbibe. These traits are not inherited, they are learned! Teach your children to treat others as they would want to be treated, with respect and we will have a shift in paradigm: a whole new world. Parents, this is on you! I have heard parents complain about the media and that some of these messages come from those external environments. Well, the culture in a home supersedes any influence of the mass media. You need to cut off those channels or avenues and give positive re-enforcements to the children. Children should be taught to embrace and celebrate our differences, rather than discriminate or bring down those different from us in race, color, gender, financial status or class and physical abilities.

Reflection

There was one in my 9th grade who I remember so clearly.

We called her "Goliath" because she was so huge! She would take your food, your money and send you on all sorts of errands, and make you serve corporal punishment. "Goliath" was involved in a fight almost every week. And she had a pack of faithful followers that clung to her like bees to honey. She was also "blessed" with a deep baritone voice that could reverberate over a distance.

One day after morning mass, we heard shouts coming from down the cafeteria. When we got to the venue of commotion, we saw "Goliath" on the floor and pounding away at her, was one of the very quiet, very tiny, principal honor's roll girls. She beat "Goliath" up and when the sisters came and queried, everyone lied that it was "Goliath" who had started the fight and beat her up.

The sisters were confused, but they had to send "Goliath" out from the boarding house. I asked the quiet girl latter how she got the "testicular fortitude" to confront "Goliath"? She said she had had enough of "Goliath" picking on her and even though she felt she was walking into a lion's den, had decided that enough was enough! "You only live and die once!" she concluded.

I am not encouraging retaliation. If you can report to a teacher, or counselor, please do so.

With counseling, many bullies have adjusted to social life and become defenders of other girls. Bullies need help. If you find yourself being mean to other girls, aggressive and physically abusive, check yourself. This is a serious disorder.

- **Attention Deficit Hyperactivity Disorder (ADHD):** This is easy to see in some girls who are simply hyper active. They are unable to sit still and become disruptive in class. They have short attention spans, become easily bored and/or frustrated with tasks. Many of them are quite intelligent, but their lack of focus frequently results in poor grades and difficulties in school.

They are impulsive, constantly moving, running, climbing, squirming, and fidgeting. They have trouble with motor skills and may be physically clumsy and awkward. Please don't make fun of anyone who exhibits these traits. They need help.

Other physical handicaps: Yes, there are special children who suffer some physical challenges and other children make it hard for them to adjust or fit into normal age-appropriate processes. Down's syndrome, sickle cell anemia, born with a cleft, born with a hole in the heart, born blind, or lame, or dumb and many more handicaps. This is how I see physical disability. A physical challenge means you have been singled out to supersede the ordinary. It means you have been destined to be a diamond in the wrought. Actually, most people have some sort of challenge or another, but they live with it, and handle it. Some of the world's greatest people, scientists, geniuses, athletes , have at one time or another, been diagnosed as having a challenge, or a physical/

mental disability. But they showed the world that the only one who can determine your future is YOU. Let no one limit what you think or know you can achieve.

Sexual Self-Awareness. During teenage years, as girls begin to realize their unique features and they also become adventurous. Some girls indulge in sexual experimentations with those of same sex. In some cases, it ends as a one-time experience that dies once self awareness and self identity kicks in. In some other girls, these tendencies remain and continue even in adulthood. In an all- girls school, this is pretty common. There is a difference between simple adventurism and a state of the search for sexual identity or plain confusion.

Some girls grapple with these feelings as some feel trapped in their physical frame or bound by cultural and societal expectations of who they should be, sexually. It is at this stage that a sexual identity crisis may occur: being gay, lesbian, or straight. Culture, the Media, and religion go a long way to determine the resolution of these feelings and emotions. Some girls are also born with male reproductive parts and suffer mental trauma trying to identify who they truly are. Many corrective surgical processes exist to help these cases. No matter what these outcome may be, remember to treat all children with love, kindness and understanding.

Peer Pressure

Young girls and teenagers are constantly under pressure, being so impressionable and adventurous. As a young girl, you may just be making your own friends and coming into awareness of yourself. You want to be liked by people. Everyone wants to "belong". You want to be seen hanging around the happening crowd, the hip group, and sometimes to belong to these groups, you may have to behave in a certain way or do certain things, Sometimes, it's just merely craving for acceptance and friends that makes you keep certain friendships. Pressure from peers who usually happen to be in the same age bracket, comes when they make you or exert enough influence on you to do something.

Peer pressure means being coerced into doing something by friends even when you think or know otherwise. This is basically because people come from different backgrounds and families. Their socio-economic spheres are very different and unique and so based on what they know, they may try to influence you to become like them. Peer pressure could be good or bad. If it is a positive thing, then that will be good pressure. Examples are children who do very well in school urging their friends to step up, girls teaching good etiquette to others who may not have had such education, moral influence, physical or good sportsman achievement, positive spiritual influence etc. Good peer pressure does not get as much recognition as bad.

What is bad peer pressure?

Following the pack in doing bad things, e.g. loss of focus, negative influence, drugs, alcohol, stealing, lying, prostitution, delinquency, etc.

Why do girls still fall into bad groups? They may be unable to stand up to people and maintain control, they lack the ability to turn away and do what they know is right. This is mainly as a result of low self-esteem which typically affects a significant percentage of teenage girls. Low self esteem is a serious problem and through teenage years continues to affect young girls resulting in drugs, suicide, sex, and more.

- Decide who makes it into your circle of friends and think before deciding.
- Think deeply too before doing things that these "friends" ask you to do, whether you want to do it, whether you should, and finally think about the consequences.
- Girls who are bad influence always seem to be popular and if you do not have solid and strong grounding, you may get tempted to join them. It is best to stay away from them. In life, there is right and wrong, good or bad, and every decision has a consequence.

Peer pressure continues into young adulthood.

- **Dealing with disagreements:**

  You will get into differences of opinions with your friends. And you will deal with arguments, quarrels and fits. It is a natural process.

- Don't let it eat you up. It is always better things over at a good time, explaining your point, or what the person did that hurt you, rather than letting it fester and it becomes a grudge. Grudges are destroyers.

- And sometimes, you may have to part ways with friends. It may hurt, but it is a part of life. It is not all the friends you start life with that you continue with or end up with.

- **Coping with a loss.** This can be very traumatic for a teenager to deal with. Sometimes we lose our friends or parents through the severing of relationships or death and we wonder why. Death has nothing to do with age. It can happen anytime, through any means. It is also a natural process of life. Yes, to lose loved ones hurts a great deal and it is good to grieve and cry and let the emotions out.

Drinks, Drugs & Sex

Reflection.

I remember while growing up in that beautiful catholic convent, we had girls who would "jump" the school fence at night to go out to attend parties with boys. They came back to tell tales, and some of those who did not have the courage to venture out sat and listened to their stories of boys, sex, drugs and life outside the pearly walls. We knew the names of the "hip" boys from other schools.

Then a sad incident happened that threw the school into a serious panic. A young girl was caught by the janitor as she came back from a party while trying to "scale" (jump) the fence. She was stone drunk and passed out in his arms.

The next time she came to herself was in the school's health clinic and that was not all. She was shamefully paraded on the assembly ground for all to see. We found out later that she had been gang raped by the boys who dumped her outside by the fence. She said she had been drugged and did not remember what had happened. She was trying to "belong". She is still alive today.

- Drinks and drugs sometimes go hand in hand with peer pressure and socializing.

- Usually occurs when hanging out with friends, at bars or at clubs.

- Drinks and drugs make you feel more relaxed, confident, and less inhibited.

- Drugs have the same effects. Examples of drugs are marijuana, (Indian hemp), big ones like ecstasy (E, MDMA), cocaine (coke, Charlie, blow) heroin, and amphetamines (speed)

- Drugs vary greatly in strength and the effect that they can have on you. Some drugs are depressants (like alcohol), and make you drowsy and more relaxed. Marijuana falls into this class. Marijuana is one of the most common drugs used by teens and is often perceived to be relatively safe, but this isn't necessarily the case.

- Alcohol is a depressant. This means that it temporarily slows down your central nervous system (the brain and the spinal cord) and therefore prevents clear transmission of messages to your brain. This slows all your bodily reactions, giving you the feeling of relaxation and decreased anxiety. Because alcohol relaxes, it is common for people to run into trouble when drunk, getting into fights or accidents.

- Stimulants make you feel more awake, alert, and give you loads of energy. Ecstasy, speed and cocaine are examples of stimulants. They increase your body temperature and blood pressure and when taken in high dosage, can make you confused, have a heart attack or even suffer brain damage.

- Heroin is one of the strongest and most dangerous drugs available. It is highly addictive and easy to overdose on often leading to death. Many TV personalities' deaths have been linked to an overdose in drugs.

It is easy to feel pressured into trying alcohol, drugs and sex by friends. Sometimes, friends get into mischief and you could get hurt. To be safe, *(hint, hint!)* when you go to parties, make sure you never leave your drink unattended. If you do have to leave it for a while, give it to a friend that you know and trust. Don't swap or share drinks and think twice about accepting a drink from someone you don't know well.

If you suddenly start to feel unusually drunk or unwell without knowing why, it is possible that your drink has been spiked. Ask a trustworthy friend to help you get away or drive you home. In the same way, if one of your friends starts acting strangely, keep an eye on them.

SAY NO TO DRUGS! I do not endorse drug use by anyone. It is a silent killer of teenagers. Some teenagers get caught up in cult activities or fraternities that use drugs, bully others or carry out murder threats.

Prostitution. Some young girls have sex for money. Sex with anyone for monetary benefits is prostitution. Greed, lack of contentment and low-self esteem are some other reasons for prostitution. The girls feel a certain pseudo "power" or "control" because their bodies are "wanted". Girls who come from abusive homes where there is lack of love or positive strong parental influence often stray into prostitution. Prostitution is as old as civilization. It is scary what those who inadvertently get lured into it go through. Many are murdered in the process; others are scared, damaged and destroyed for life.

On the internet, many web sites pop up with prostitutes wanting to "Chat" on "hot lines" while many of these young girls become pornographic video stars.

"News broke Tuesday that a prolific porn actor had tested positive for HIV.... By Pandora Young on October 14, 2010 2:54 PM" http://www.mediabistro.com

It is terrible that some sick minded people use young children for some of these videos. This is wrong and should be seriously legislated by the government.

Reflection.

It is shameful that some men and even parents encourage these young girls to do this. During that eventful trip to Nigeria where I met Rita, all the young girls and their parents wanted was for me was to take their children abroad! Some openly said the girls should go "use what they have to get what they want"? You find young girls canvassing hotel rooms, hunting for men. There are also the pimps hanging around hotels with pictures of different girls and who know the telephone numbers of the rich and famous. They organize all kinds of "parties" where they parade the girls to prospective clients.

Girls, you are worth more than this. It should be more about what you have in your head and heart and not about your body. By learning an early skill set, you can engage in some honest means of income. Greed is what causes most young girls to prostitute because you want to buy clothes, travel, buy houses and estates and be seen with the "crowd".

Another group gets into prostitution to survive from poverty.

Sexual Abuse and Rape

There are so many stories every day about young girls being raped. Vulnerable young girls and children are often victims of this terrible thing. It is a very scary and traumatic thing.

- Rape is a situation where a person forces you to have sex.

- People that violate innocent defenseless are called pedophiles. In some countries, they are sent to jail when caught for this heinous crime.

- There have been cases of children who died after the ordeal.

- In some communities, children are molested and nothing happens to the predator. Minor children must be protected by the legal arms of any government.

- Rape happens every second to a young child, a young girl and it is by "familiar" persons. This means in your household: uncles, cousins, fathers and even mothers are abusing someone else.

- Most of the males are role models. Financial care givers, supporters of the family, step fathers, teachers, principals, bosses at work, and these men have a control over their vulnerable victims and use their position of power to oppress them.

- Children bold enough to speak may not be believed. They are threatened and keep quiet out of fear. Society makes it impossible for a young girl to speak out. It is wrong, condemnable and every parent and family member should be aware that it exists, even within their family. Parents are most culpable of being quiet when this type of thing happens.

Reflection

I saw a Hindu movie called "Monsoon wedding". A character serially raped young girls in his family and no one said anything about his crime because of his perceived influential position in the family.

Consider the 2009 CNN reported case of the 8 year old Liberian girl in the USA reported to have been raped by her cousins. Her parents and family were very angry and said it was her fault and she had brought them shame; they abandoned this child who had to be taken into the Arizona child protection service.

Consider the recent case of the Australian man, Josef Fritzl, who fathered children by his own daughter and kept her locked in the basement!

In some cultures, girls as young as 10 years old are given in marriage to men old enough to be their fathers. These men rape these children and have babies by these babies. Most of the girls end up with V.V.F. (Vesicovaginal Fistula) where the young immature bodies and bladder of these girls get severely damaged by pregnancy and the girls lose continence.

Some poverty-stricken young girls, children, and even toddlers in third world nations, are forced to earn a living by hawking or selling goods. In some cases, they are kidnapped and used as sex slaves or smuggled out of their countries to be used as prostitutes.

In some schools, you find teachers abusing or victimizing students by threatening to give them poor grades if they do not give in. As a college student, you need to ensure that you study very hard and you know you have mastered the course. If any lecturer attempts to victimize you, you have the right to seek redress immediately. You can report to the education board. If you are confident you have done your part and you answered accurately, you will be bold enough to shout to high heavens.

In South Africa, there was a myth peddled by cross section of ill-educated miscreants that if you slept with a virgin, you would be cured of AIDS. This led to an increased incidence of the rape of young girls. Thankfully, this situation has been addressed.

Rape can also happen between dating partners or two acquaintances, or it could be with someone you were already sexually involved with, and minimal pain or violence may be involved.

"Date rape" drugs take as little as 15 minutes to kick in and can wipe out your memory for an eight hour period, leaving you open to sexual assault and rape. (An example is the celebrated case of the heir to multi-billion empire of Max Factor).

Prevention.

Rape happens very fast and so one must be fully aware and alert and be prepared to prevent it from happening.

- The moment a situation becomes uncomfortable, stop, speak up, or leave.
- If you don't feel right and your brain is telling you that you may be getting into a bad situation, walk away.
- Young girls should not be found in compromising situations like being cajoled to go to parties, going into hotels with men, being alone with bosses, drinking or going under the influence of drugs or alcohol or dressing provocatively.
- Don't engage in "Sexting" pornography and using modern IT social networks and internet to meet or chat with people. Don't forget that there are many sick psychopaths out there and you may be talking to one of them. Many young children have been molested by people they started corresponding with via the internet so parents, beware.

Rape leaves a grave effect on a child. Feelings of being dirty, unclean, ashamed, guilty, not worthy, suicidal, depressed, repellent, angry and lots more. They go through a myriad of physical evaluations. There are girls who have developed STDs and some children have been born out of rape incidents.

Physical, Mental and Practical defense for girls.

1. Never be intimidated. Avoid uncompromising situations. Never allow yourself to get isolated by anyone. Don't live in fear. You are not a weak, powerless person .Always draw on your strength by being mentally prepared to defend yourself. Use your brains: stay calm, do not get into verbal quarrels. Most fights are won before they start, and aggressors will back down if you maintain eye contact and are not intimidated by them. Have you ever observed the hypnotic gaze of the cobra as he zeroes down on his victim? It never takes its eyes off the target. Never turn your back on your assailant.

2. Stay aware of people in your surroundings. Attackers or predators always survey the terrain before they strike. Pay attention! Who is looking at you? Watch!

3. Stay within a crowded environment. Except in cases where girls have been gang-raped, rape occurs in isolated environs. Do not ever let yourself be taken somewhere.

4. Attract attention. When predators get to their prey, they use the "paralysis syndrome" of fear. The male tells you not to scream or he will kill you, or in the case of repeated molestation says you are not to tell anyone. He's telling you exactly what will ruin his plan, so go ahead, ruin his plan -- create a disturbance, scream, and tell people who know him. Some will believe, some won't but that would put a stop to his plan.

5. Control his hips and his hands. If you can get your feet on his hips you can control the distance between the two of you. His hands are the weapons he will use against you. He will hit you, slap you, stab you or shoot you, but he has to use his hands to do the damage.

6. Contrary to your instincts, running away isn't always the best solution. If there is no where to get help nearby there is a good chance your attacker will catch up with you: watch all these horror movies and see how many girls escape. But run if there is a way to get help in sight or if you've physically disabled your attacker enough to get away.

7. Other ways may include making a quick run and having your phone on speed dial for emergency. Leave your phone on even if you are attacked, that way the other person on the line can hear

you. Try to describe where you are for them in clues or codes. If you know the attacker, call their name several times.

8. In case it is an attack in your home, for those who have it, use your viewer to see who is outside before you open the door; never let someone in if you feel uneasy about them, particularly if you are alone. Children must be taught never to let anyone into the home without permission. In areas where 911 works, make sure children know how to call for help.

9. Some people can sense when someone has been in their home, or space. You get "goose bumps" or a chill running down your spine because your guts tell you. It may be carelessly placed furniture as a tell-tale sign. Whatever it is, walk out of the house immediately.

10. Read, read, and read. Study trends of rape victims and cases and learn from other people's experiences

Target areas for attack

- Eyes, throat, groin, face, abdomen using your elbows, knees, head and teeth. We have seen movies of how a woman can bring a man down by a calculated kick of the knee on the groin area.

- Knees – A woman's legs are the strongest part of her body. The area around the kneecap can do unthinkable damage when brought up between an attacker's legs. Aim at the testicles with your knees.

- Head – The skull is made of very hard bone. Usually women are smaller than their assailants, so using the head for a head-butt or slamming into the face can cause a lot of pain.
- Feet: use your heel to stomp down on their toes
- Teeth – Bite, bite and bite. Take off skin. It takes no training to know how to bite, and a bite will hurt no matter where it's placed.
- Eyes –Use anything you have to poke at the eyes. A pencil, pin, bottle… If an attacker grabs you it means his hands are occupied. With you free hand, grab his neck, wrap your fingers around his ear and grind your thumb into the eye. Show no mercy and be committed 100%. This is a survival for life and if he had his way, you will be dead.
- Throat- is very delicate. Kick the neck or grab the windpipe as if clutching and squeezing your fist and pull out with force.

3.

~

THE ULTIMATE WOMAN.....WHO AM I.......

You may be grasping with an identity issue. Who am I?

Who am I plagues the mind of almost everybody. What is my cause? Why was I born? Why into this family? Why on this side of the world? What makes me think? What forms the essence of this "being" that looks into a mirror and knows I am me? How did I get here? Where did I come from? How do I achieve all my dreams, goals and aspirations?

This is the process of self-identity which quite a lot of teenage girls battle with. Why do you want to be someone else? I hear girls say, "oh, I wish I was Halle Berry" or some celebrity that they admire. You don't know what that person goes through..he who wears the shoe knows how it hurts! Be comfortable in yourself and be proud of who you are.

You must realize that the creator has made you special, with a special mission, and given each of us unique talents that are as unique as our fingerprints.

Girl, "you are wonderfully and fearfully made" and you can be the next female president or business mogul. It depends on you,

You have the option to go left or right, to stay right or go wrong, and there are no in-betweens. There are no grey areas. You can become another Hitler, Napoleon or another Gandhi or Mother Theresa. At the end of the day, it rests solely with you to determine what you shall become.

Choices we make form the backbone of our structure in life and we must be ready to face consequences from every decision taken. There is price for every time we have to make a choice. Always.

Your decision, as a youth, would go a long way into paving the path that leads to either success in life or failure as a productive member of society.

What are the indicatives? If you continue on the path of idlers who only want to party all day and all night rather than read, who want to smoke crack at indiscreet places, who want to dress up half-naked and roam the streets aimlessly, who only want to talk about boys, fast deals, quick deals and scams, then expect the "great "fall out.

If you hang around and imbibe lessons from studious, fastidious, hard-working, honest, dependable, collected and coordinated people, expect the results. Often in our later years, we say "if only I could turn back the hands of time" well you cannot. Period! It's gone.

Constantly, there is a fight of good and evil thoughts in your mind. You have to fight hard, constantly and kill those negative thoughts.

And you under estimate how strong you are! Your will power, your determination, aggressiveness in pursuit, your ability to take all the "NO"s and keep on! That is the difference between those that fail and those that succeed.

You find that drugs, sex outside marriage, pornography look like fun, but they will surely lead you to self-destruct. Where there is a desire, the mind sees an opening, a need, a want, an enticement and at this point, you must decide.

I want to recant the story of Dr. Faustus and Mephistopheles written by Christopher Marlowe.

Dr. Faustus was a brilliant magician, but desired more magical powers and Mephistopheles offered it to him, at a price. A blood covenant!

He would only live for a certain period with the greatest power the world has ever seen. Dr. Faustus signed the agreement with the blood covenant. Dr. Faustus achieved fame and fortune, beyond his expectations. He enjoyed himself immensely and totally forgot the contract. Finally, the day of reckoning drew near and Mephistopheles appeared to remind him. Faustus became aggrieved and started pleading, but it was too late. He had signed the contract and he had to pay.

Such is the pact many of us may have signed unwittingly with the types of evil things we indulge in. We must pay the price!

Today is a new day, a new beginning, a re-birth, a new birth! You can start today to remake the rest of your life!

Reflection

As a teenager, I was in the limelight. Been a top model, been on TV, faced bad and good paparazzi, and was regarded as a relatively privileged teen from a good societal background. I moved within high social class because of what I was doing and who I was. I was recognized everywhere I went to and was, a national celebrity. Yet day in, day out, I still felt a void. Even with the parties and fun, there was that deep, dark and dreadful void. I started drinking bottles of wine: just to get rid of the loneliness. I was lonely and alone, even in the crowd. Now, I realize I was on the verge of depression.

Then life started to unfold gradually. Good friends started dying, and I started realizing that death did not only affect very old people. I wondered about eternity, and frankly, hell! I believe at this point was my period of turn around: A 360 degrees change.

I started prioritizing things, studying hard at school, cutting back on bad friends and parties, re-focused my mind on God, family, career and the opportunity to give back.

Today, you have the opportunity of making things right.

And I do not believe we go through situations coincidentally, but to use it as a teachable moment. We are meant to go through them to learn and be stronger when we get out of it.

So there is a plan for you but sometimes, you must be purged like silver through fire so that even when challenges come, you strive on. Without obstacles or challenges, how can one conquer, without a war, where is the victory? Without testing silver through fire, where would the purity come from?

The future is in your hands.

You must say "NO" to things that threaten to bring you down,

You must forgive others and yourselves from our past sins. Forgive yourself and release yourself to enter into a new you. Consider it like the molting of a snake, like the re-birth of dead cells in our bodies; consider that for a seed to germinate and bring forth new life, it must first die. Something must give. Something must die.

You must forge new alliances made up of self-motivated people who can help you accomplish your vision and stay away from whiners and negative thinkers. They are like dead-weight anchors, dragging us into the abyss of death. Let go of them.

You must feed the mind, constantly. A popular adage we had in college was RIRO: Rubbish in, Rubbish out. If you put rubbish of pornography and cursing and internet surfing into your mind, that is what usually seeps out. The mind is a terrible thing to waste. There are no short cuts in life: to be successful, you have to work hard. You must use the growth of a plant as an analogy.

You first till the soil, before you plant. You then water the plant and watch it grow. You prune around it to endure it does not get choked by weeds; you water it constantly and add fertilizer. It does not grow overnight: it take a while before the season of harvest. But if you have done your work right, you will reap the harvest!

So let's put down some very important lessons on growing up.

1.   Accountability, Responsibility and Organization:

These three factors are very important in the growth of any young girl.

Responsibility affects the manner and way you conduct yourself. You have to be matured in your ways and level of reasoning. No longer do you get angry, agitated, aggressive and ill-tempered. Maturity means being calm in the face of anything and listening to a voice of reasoning with respect of other people's perspective of things. It is no longer " Your way, or the highway" Responsibility means knowing what is right from wrong and choosing to do right. Responsibility says I can accept it when I have done wrong and can take corrections. It means knowing what to do, when, how, why and where to do it.

Organization means you have to prioritize and have order in your life. It signifies that in every 24 hours, you must know what you will be doing at every hour that would move your life forward positively. It means setting goals, methods and phases in achieving those goals. It means you must have an immediate, short, and long term goal in life. This means, no matter where you are right now in life, begin to plot how you and where you wish to position yourself in the next 2 years, 5 years and 10 years. You can then start working diligently towards those goals and get the tools to accomplish them. If you fail to plan, you plan to fail. You must be prepared to do the small hard things now, so as to reap a great harvest in future.

It means having a "To Do" list on a daily basis and keeping non-productive activities out of your list. Organization means there is enough time in one day, but you must understand time management.

Organization also means you must know where and how you store up and keep your things in the order that you will remember and will be easy to find.

You must learn to balance a check book and basic business administration. You must know and understand the power and value of money. You must know what you need, what you want, understand basic economic principles of opportunity cost, scale of preferences, capital, resources, and profit and loss. You have to learn how to write out business plans and proposals. You have to learn marketing strategies and what is called "The spill" which is a 1-2 minute rehearsed speech about who you are, what you do, and how you can be a valuable asset to any business.

2. Resourcefulness: In most communities, women are made to feel second placed to men. This mental psychological abuse is passed on to their daughters. No girl or woman is second class to any man. We are imbued with the same talents and intelligence. Unfortunately, societal laws make it tougher and harsher for women to succeed at ventures that they embark on while the men have it easier. This is not to start a war on the sexes. Throughout history, women have been deeply marginalized and same obtain till date. Despite this, there are so many case of women who have risen above and gone beyond these societal and gender boundaries to become the best. What this simply means is that women have to be ten times more hardworking, more resourceful, more dedicated, more focused in these hostile environments by bracing up to the challenges with an "I can do it" attitude.

3. Expectations: You must know and realize your potentials and not be ready to settle for less. What do you expect from yourself? What does your culture or society expect from you? An African adage goes like this, "Train a woman, you train a nation" How ready are you? Women not only nurture and raise the family, providing emotional and psychological stability, they are also bread winners! Women are multi-tasking.

Only a woman can be braiding hair, cooking and mixing ingredients on the stove, doing home work and sorting laundry while talking or giving instructions on the phone! Our brains are wired specially and there is a reason for that. A woman has to play so many roles in life. She is mother to her children, wife and mother to her husband, therapist, cleaner, cook, provider, doctor, plumber, cheerleader, driver, counselor, and through it all, she is expected to smile and be courteous, humble, gracious, helpful, forging, loyal, faithful and strong. Only a woman can effectively juggle running a home and being owner of a business. You see why we need more female leaders and presidents?

4. Determination and Purpose: Right from the beginning, you must set your goals and strive towards them with determination and purpose, realizing that nothing good comes easy in life. Like said previously, life throws many detours in our way and your ability to remain focused with perseverance and relentlessness will make the difference between you and others. With tenacity and focus, you will attain whatever goals you determine in life.

5. Learn to build on your strengths. As you go on in life, you will identify areas of strengths and weaknesses. Don't let the

weaknesses get you down, but zero in on the strengths and continue to use them. Accentuate your good sides, always.

Also do things with confidence. Once you always feel good about yourself, knowing that you can achieve anything you dream of, that you will get many "Nos" and some "Yes", you will be alright. Everyone cannot see your dreams as you do. YOU see the dreams and that's all that matters! This even affects your dressing or make-up. Learn your body type and what looks best on you. You do not need to follow fashion blindly but learn what works best for you.

6. Take criticisms well and learn from them. Don't start sulking when someone points out an error; instead be happy for the opportunity to be corrected into becoming a better person. No one has all the knowledge in the world.

7. Learn to talk about things. There is really no big deal to anything. If you as a girl can learn to talk about things and not wallow in the emotions, no matter the outcome, you may learn that there is nothing new under the sun. It helps to talk to someone older, particularly about very emotional stuff. Sex, drugs, boys, bullying, suicide, these things have been going on since the beginning of creation and will go on after we are long gone. Like

the bible says, "there is nothing new under the sun." We must learn to open up and talk about them.

8. Appreciation and gratitude for whatever people do for you. Teens sometimes have an "entitlement" mentality. Well, you need to be grateful for anything you get in life. There are some words that will help you get along in life. "Thank you" and "I am sorry". These words we learned as toddlers, yet they continue to help in life.

9. Leadership skills. At this age, you should get involved in scholarly debates, political and current affairs, law and ethics, arts, medicine, field trips, musicals, engineering, mentoring, volunteering and other areas of endeavor that will equip you for the future leader that you will be. Read about past leaders and times of challenges they had to deal with so that you can be better prepared.

Mentoring and giving back are crucial principles to imbibe at this stage. You must begin to think of how you can and should make your world a better place. You must think of giving back to the community and the type of legacy you hope to leave for the future. It is building blocks, one step at a time, and one block at a time. The world waits for you: you are the hope of the future...be excited about what a huge impact YOU will have on the world!

10. Get an education! It is an absolute necessity in today's world. Sure, you can be a famous actress, sure you can be a rapper, sure you can be an athlete, but all these things can be taken from you in a flash. You will shine for a while and wane, slowly. So you must always prepare your plan B or your exit strategy. Nobody can take your education from you. It is your power, it is your ammunition. And really, if you know how to make money, but don't know how to count or save and invest it, you will soon be poor. It's what Will Smith calls the "poverty mentally" always thinking of spending and buying "blink blink" to impress and be living like the Jones and never thinking of the future.

Look at all the top artists of today. Many of them are dying broke! Some have major issues with the IRS and some cannot even balance their check books. Why? Many did not get the appropriate education to teach them about managing their money.

You must go through formal education to learn mathematics, statistic, calculus, the science, history, government. Barack Obama did not become president by chance. He went through school. He went through Harvard. He learned and studied about world economics and governance in international relations and diplomacy. You cannot become your dream by chance, you must work in a calculated way, train like a soldier preparing for war, and for a woman, an education is an absolute.

11. Self-Sacrifice. There is a process to follow in the growth chart. First is self-indulgence, then self-awareness and finally, self-sacrifice. Once you realize and you have grown from being a child who is demanding, selfish, self-centered, you get to the stage of conflict. This is where you grapple with your role in this world and finally, comes the ultimate self-sacrifice part where you have come full circle in knowing that your calling is not all about you, but about the change that you can make, selflessly. As a woman, you are challenged by religion, culture and historical depictions or expectations of your role which could be limiting. You fight more battles based on your gender than more and this continues throughout life. This gender inequality led to the 70s burning of the bra phase when women said "NO" to inequalities. But let us prepare for the challenge and the war will be easier. Preparation comes by being better than the rest. In developing nations, women are subject to more inequalities than other places. If you are in such regions, know that you are

the hope for the world and unborn generation. You could change the course of history by hard work, fearlessness, education, and a refusal to be intimidated by others who want to use your gender to bring you down.

12. Align with like minds and seek those who know more. It is a sad person that surrounds himself with only those inferior to him. What can he learn?

Enjoy life..Live, love and laugh...enjoy your teen years because when they go..they go...they are gone...forever..you can only be 13 or 16 once! You can never get it back. You must enjoy every moment; enjoy friends, family and the opportunities you have to learn. Don't take yourself so seriously that you forget how to enjoy what every moment brings. And don't forget, every emotion depends on your perspective of the presenting situation, so learn to look on the brighter side of life. See humor in things, don't be a "wet blanket" Everyone likes a witty, amiable, easy- to -get -along person. You must be comfortable with who you are; in your skin, your gender, your sexuality, your personality and your family background. There are no two people like you in this world; no Siamese twins or clones. You are unique and special and so you are wonderfully different from others.

You do not need to be someone else to feel good within yourself. You have no cause to be ashamed of who you are, except you know you have broken some laws. Then get over it quickly and bounce back by making amends and looking forward. You must take pride in what you have accomplished so far in life, where you know you are going and who you know you will become by various ongoing experiences.

13. Do away with bad habits and poor choices or decisions. They will get you killed. Texting while driving is responsible for the deaths of many teens. Driving under the influence will get you into BIG trouble, going into places with strangers and not telling anyone because you are now a "big girl", sleeping with multiple partners, having no future goals or ambition with a burning desire to achieve it and succeed, living with fear in an abusive relationship, having no religious foundation or grounding so that you practically have no spiritual or moral values, placing no value in relationships or losing the value of one-to –one human contact...these are dangerous practices for teenager.

The internet and technology has made teenagers go into a cocoon where they stay. You all are hooked on your iPods, telephones, computers, surfing, chatting, emailing and texting. What ever happened to good old plain human conversations? Imagine this.. two people in the same room, sending text messages?

Finally....pray, pray and pray first. Depending on your religious inclination, it always pays to be grounded in a belief-system. For Christians, the bible forms solid bedrock for success and amicable existence with others in life. The teachings, the spiritual benefits continuously prune you and make you a better human being. A warning to fellow parents: guide your utterances and words from your mouth. You will get what you asked for. If you profess negativity into your child, that is what he or she will become. You must make it a conscious effort to bless your teenager, no matter how she behaves. Words are life and there is power in the tongue. According to Pastor Kevin of 12 stones church, there are 5 key elements of parental blessing.

a. You must have a meaningful physical touch with your child; be it a rub of the shoulders or a simple hug. It forever blesses the child in his memories.

b. Like said earlier, chose the right spoken words to speak life into your child.

c. Attach very high value and importance to them. They mean more than anything else and come first.

d.   Picture a special future for them and where you see them positioned in life. Picture it and claim it.

e.   Make an active effort and commitment to fulfill their blessing.

CLOSING REMARKS: So is there an alien?

Teenagers want to be understood. They need to be informed about life, their parents need to speak truthfully about events, phases and life as it actually obtains. Parents and teenagers alike should not view each other as the enemy or foreigner. Teenagers, your parents love you and really want the best for you. They do not want you to make the same mistakes that they perhaps made. Maybe we can sit down and simply talk with openness, frankness and honesty. The young girl is the soul of any nation and must be equipped, prepared and positioned to take over the reins of leadership. She must be empowered to know who she is in her culture, society and family. She is not a 2nd class citizen. She goes through a lot physically, mentally and psychologically and must be given the right tools to navigate life. The education of girls determines the future of any nation.

Texting words teenagers use.

Yes!! There is communication within the alien space! L.O.L.

For you to communicate there must be an understanding of the words, lingo, idioms and other non-conventional methods of communication. The important thing is that the message sent is accurately decoded.

A friend who has 2 adult and 2 teenage children complained to me during the course of writing this book that he felt like an alien in his own house. He said," I cannot understand what they are saying. It's like they are from space or another planet, speaking gibberish. What can I do because they make me feel old and uncomfortable? They are speaking in "tongues" or codes or in a language I cannot decipher."

Well, here is the answer! Text codes and short hands. If you can understand this, then you can unravel, to an extent, the teenage language. But you have to increase your speed because teenagers are so fast!

5FS = 5 Finger Salute

H4XX0R = a "hacker" or "to be hacked"

ABITHIWTIDB = A bird In The Hand Is Worth Two In The Bush

AFAHMASP = A Fool And His Money Are Soon Parted

AFPOE = A Fresh Pair Of Eyes

AFAGAY = A Friend As Good As You

AFINIAFI = A Friend In Need Is A Friend Indeed

ABT2 = About To

AWOL = Absent Without Leave

ACK = Acknowledgement

ALTG = Act Locally, Think Globally

ALOL = Actually Laughing Out Loud

ADR = Address

AAS = Alive And Smiling

Alcon = All Concerned

OK = All Correct

ADBB = All Done Bye Bye

AMBW = All My Best Wishes

AML = All My Love

AMRMTYFTS = All My Roommates Thank You For The Show

AOAS = All Of A Sudden

ATW = All the Web or Around the Web

AYCE = All You Can Eat

aight = Alright

AKA or a.k.a. = Also Known As

AATK = Always At The Keyboard

AIMP = Always In My Prayers

ALOTBSOL = Always Look On The Bright Side Of Life

AAAAA = American Association Against Acronym Abuse

AGKWE = And God Knows What Else

ANFSCD = And Now For Something Completely Different

AYTMTB = And You're Telling Me This Because

ADAD = Another Day Another Dollar

ADIH = Another Day In Hell

ADIP = Another Day In Paradise

AND = Any day now

NESEC = Any Second

NE1 = Anyone

NE1ER = Anyone Here

NE = Anyway

AWGTHTGTTA = Are We Going To Have To Go Through This Again

RU = Are You

RUNTS = are you Nuts?

RUOK = Are you OK

RUT = aRe yoU There?

RUUP4IT = Are You Up For It

AYC = Aren't You Clever -or- Aren't You Cheeky

AAF = As A Friend

AAMOF = As A Matter Of Fact

AAMOI = As A Matter Of Interest

AAYF = As Always, Your Friend

AEAP = As Early As Possible

AFIAA = As Far As I Am Aware

AFAICS = As Far As I Can See

AFAICT = As far As I can Tell

AFAIK = As Far As I Know

AFAIU = As Far As I Understand

AFAIUI = As Far As I Understand It

AFAIC = As Far As I'm Concerned

AFAP = As Far As Possible

AFAYC = As Far As You're Concerned

AIMB = As I Mentioned Before

AISB = As I Said Before

AISE = As I Said Earlier

AISI = As I See It

AIH = As It Happens

ALAP = As Late As Possible

AMAP = As Many As Possible

ASAP = As Soon As Possible

AYK = As You Know

AAK = Asleep At Keyboard

AAR = At Any Rate

AAR8 = At Any Rate

@TEOTD = At The End Of The Day

ATST = At The Same Time

AFC = Away From Computer

AFK = Away From Keyboard -or- A Free Kill

BAK = Back At my Keyboard

BITD = Back In The Day

BIF = Basis In Fact or Before I Forget

BR = Bathroom

BB = Be Back

BBIAB = Be Back In A Bit

BBIAF = Be Back In A Few

BBIAS = Be Back In A Sec

BBIAW = Be Back In A While

BBL = Be Back Later

BBSD = Be Back Soon Darling

BBSL = Be Back Sooner or Later

BBT = Be Back Tomorrow

BRB = Be Right Back

BRT = Be Right There

BCNU = Be Seein' You

B/C = Because

BCOZ = Because

BNDN = Been Nowhere Done Nothing

BTDT = Been There Done That

BTDTGTS = Been There, Done That, Got The T-shirt

BIBO = Beer In, Beer Out

B4 = Before

B4U = Before You

B4YKI = Before You Know It

BL = Belly Laughing

BOHICA = Bend Over Here It Comes Again

BFF = Best Friends Forever

BFFTTE = Best Friends Forever Til The End

BW = Best Wishes

BKA = Better Known As

BHAG = Big Hairy Audacious Goal

BHG = Big Hearted Guy -or- Big Hearted Girl

BNF = Big Name Fan

BPLM = Big Person Little Mind

BSAAW = Big Smile And A Wink

BWO = Black, White or Other

BIOYE = Blow It Out Your Ear

BIOYIOP = Blow It Out Your I/O Port

BIOYN = Blow it Out Your Nose

BSBD&NE; = Book Smart, Brain Dead & No Experience

BYOA = Bring Your Own Advil

BO = Bug Off -or- Body Odor

BWL = Bursting With Laughter

BAU = Business As Usual

BMGWL = Busting My Gut With Laughter

BDBI5M = Busy Daydreaming Back In 5 Minutes

BOCTAAE = But Of Course There Are Always Exceptions

BOTOH = But On The Other Hand

BSF = But Seriously, Folks

BTA = But Then Again or Before The Attacks

BWDIK = But What Do I Know

BYKT = But you Knew That

BTW = By The Way

BTWITIAILW/U = By The Way I Think I Am In Love With You

BIBI = Bye Bye

BBB = Bye Bye Babe -or- Boring Beyond Belief

BBBG = Bye Bye Be Good

BBN = Bye Bye Now

B4N = Bye For Now

CFV = Call For Vote

CTA = Call To Action

CY = Calm Yourself

CBB = Can't Be Bothered

CRAT = Can't Remember A Thing

CRTLA = Can't Remember the Three-Letter Acronym

CSL = Can't Stop Laughing

COS = Change Of Subject

CB = Chat Brat -or- Coffee Break

CWYL = Chat With You Later

CRAP = Cheap Redundant Assorted Products

CYM = Check Your Mail

CTC = Choking The Chicken -or- Care To Chat

C&G; = Chuckly and Grin

CofS = Church of Scientology

C4N = Ciao For Now

C-T = City

COB = Close Of Business

CICO = Coffee In, Coffee Out

CRB = Come Right Back

gratz = Congratulations

CID = Consider It Done

CNP = Continued in Next Post

KEWL = Cool

CAAC = Cool As A Cucumber

CMIW = Correct Me if I'm Wrong

CMF = Count My Fingers

QT = Cutie

DGYF = Damn Girl You're Fine

DITR = Dancing In The Rain

DF = Dear Friend

DH = Dear Hubby or Husband

DORD = Department of Redundancy Department

DOE = Depends On Experience

DITYID = Did I Tell You I'm Distressed

DUST = Did You See That

DIKU = Do I Know You

DILLIGAD = Do I Look Like I Give A Damn

DIY = Do It Yourself

DTRT = Do The Right Thing

DYHAB = Do You Have A Boyfriend

DYHAG = Do You Have A Girlfriend

DWYM = Does What You Mean

DBA = Doing Business As

DP = Domestic Partner

DAMHIKT = Don't Ask Me How I Know That

DBEYR = Don't Believe Everything You Read

DETI = Don't Even Think It

DGA = Don't Go Anywhere

DGT = Don't Go There

DGTG = Don't Go There Girlfriend

DHYB = Don't Hold Your Breath

DKDC = Don't Know Don't Care

DLTBBB = Don't Let The Bed Bugs Bite

DLTM = Don't Lie To Me

DMI = Don't Mention It

DQYDJ = Don't Quit Your Day Job

DQMOT = Don't Quote Me On This

DRIB = Don't Read If Busy

DWBH = Don't Worry Be Happy

DWB = Don't Write Back

DYJHIW = Don't You Just Hate it When...

DL = Download -or- Dead Link

DUI = Driving Under the Influence

DWI = Driving While Intoxicated

DWS = Driving While Stupid

DARFC = Ducking And Running For Cover

DYFM = Dude You Fascinate Me

DD = Due Diligence

EZ = Easy

EML = Email Me Later

EMSG = E-Mail Message

EWI = E-mailing While Intoxicated

EOD = End Of Day

EOM = End Of Message

EOT = End Of Thread (meaning: end of discussion)

NRG = Energy

NUFF = Enough Said

ESO = Equipment Smarter than Operator

ETA = Estimated Time of Arrival

ETLA = ETLA Extended Three-Letter Acronym (that is, an FLA)

EVRE1 = Every One

ESEMED = Every Second Every Minute Every Day

EG = Evil Grin

EL = Evil Laugh

EMRTW = Evil Monkey's Rule The World

X-I-10 = Exciting

EM = Excuse Me

XME = Excuse Me

EMFBI = Excuse Me For Butting In

EMI = Excuse My Ignorance

F2F = Face-to-Face

FILTH = Failed In London, Try Hong Kong

FBKS = Failure Between Keyboard and Seat

FOMCL = Falling Off My Chair Laughing

FOFL = Falling on Floor Laughing

FMTYEWTK = Far More Than You Ever Wanted To Know

FTASB = Faster Than A Speeding Bullet

FTL = Faster Than Light

FE = Fatal Error

FUD = Fear, Uncertainty, and Disinformation

FAB = Features Attributes Benefits

FITB = Fill in the Blanks

FISH = First in, Still Here

FAWC = For Anyone Who Cares

FTLOG = For The Love Of God

FTR = For The Record

FTTB = For The Time Being

FTW = For The Win

FWIW = For What It's Worth

FYA = For Your Amusement

FYE = For Your Edification

FYI = For Your Information

FYM = For Your Misinformation

4NR = Foreigner

4ever = Forever

4EAE = ForEver And Ever

FWD = Forward

FLA = Four Letter Acronym

FOC = Free of Charge

FAQL = Frequently Asked Questions List

FF&PN; = Fresh Fields and Pastures New

FOAF = Friend Of A Friend

FF = Friends Forever

FWB = Friends With Benefits

FTBOMH = From The Bottom Of My Heart

FYLTGE = From Your Lips To Gods Ears

FBI = Fucking Brilliant Idea

GIGO = Garbage In, Garbage Out

GOS = Gay Or Straight

GLBT = Gay, Lesbian, Bisexual, Transgender

GIWIST = Gee, I Wish I'd Said That

GUD = Geographically UnDesirable

GAL = Get A Life

GALHER = Get A Load of Her

GALHIM = Get A Load of Him

GOYHH = Get Off Your High Horse

GOI = Get Over It

GWS = Get Well Soon

GTM = Giggle To Myself

GOL = Giggling Out Loud

GF = Girlfriend

GALGAL = Give A Little Get A Little

GMAB = Give Me A Break

GTSY = Glad To See You

GA = Go Ahead

GFI = Go For It

GTH = Go To Hell

GDI = God Damn It -or- God Damn Independent

GLYASDI = God Loves You And So Do I

GOK = God Only Knows

GTRM = Going To Read Mail

GFN = Gone For Now

GFTD = Gone For The Day

GL = Good Luck -or- Get Lost

GM = Good Morning

GNSD = Good Night Sweet Dreams

DOEI = Goodbye (in Dutch)

CIAO = Goodbye (in Italian)

POOF = Good-bye, also seen as ::poof::

GAP = Got A Pic?

GAS = Got A Second

GNBLFY = Got Nothing But Love For You

GTG = Got To Go

G2GLYS = Got To Go Love Ya So

GTGP = Got To Go Pee

GTGB = Got To Go, Bye

GGN = Gotta Go Now

GGP = Gotta Go Pee

GR8 = Great

GBG = Great Big Grin

GBH = Great Big Hug

GMTA = Great Minds Think Alike

GMTFT = Great Minds Think For Themselves

GR&D; = Grinning Running And Ducking

GD&R; = Grinning, Ducking and Running

G = Guess -or- Grin

HHO1/2K = Ha Ha, Only Half Kidding

HHOK = Ha Ha, Only Kidding

HHOS = Ha-Ha, Only Being Serious

HHOJ = Ha-Ha, Only Joking

HITAKS = Hang In There And Keep Smiling

HTB = Hang The Bastards

HHIS = Hanging Head In Shame

HHTYAY = Happy Holidays To You And Yours

RRR = haR haR haR (instead of LOL)

HAGN = Have A Good Night

HAGO = Have A Good One

HAGD = Have a Great Day

HAND = Have a Nice Day

HUA = Heads Up Ace

HAWTLW = Hello And Welcome To Last Week

HF = Hello Friend -or- Have Fun -or- Have Faith

HIOOC = Help, I'm Out Of Coffee

HWGA = Here We Go Again

HT = Hi There

HTNOTH = Hit The Nail On The Head

HD = Hold

h/o = Hold On

h/p = Hold Please

HOHA = HOllywood HAcker

HCC = Holy Computer Crap

HIH = Hope It Helps

HTH = Hope This (or That) Helps

HBIB = Hot But Inappropriate Boy

HNTW = How Nice That Was

HNTI = How Nice That/This Is

HSIK = How Should I Know

HIG = How's It Going

H&K; = Hug and Kiss

HUGZ = Hugs

HAK = Hugs And Kisses

XOXO = Hugs and Kisses

HB = Hurry Back

IAW = I Agree With

IASAP4U = I Always Say A Prayer For You

IANAC = I Am Not A Crook

IANADBIPOOTV = I Am Not A Doctor But I Play One On TV

IANAL = I Am Not A Lawyer

IANAE = I Am Not an Expert

IANNNGC = I Am Not Nurturing the Next Generation of Casualties

IMS = I Am Sorry

IAT = I Am Tired

IM2BZ2P = I aM Too Busy To (even) Pee!

IBTD = I Beg To Differ

ICBW = I Could Be Wrong

IDST = I Didn't Say That

IDC = I Don't Care

IDGI = I Don't Get It

IDK = I Don't Know

IDKY = I Don't Know You

IDTS = I Don't Think So

IFAB = I Found A Bug

IGTP = I Get The Point

IGGP = I Gotta Go Pee

IHA = I Hate Acronyms

IHAIM = I Have Another Instant Message

IHNO = I Have No Opinion

IHU = I Hear You

IKALOPLT = I Know A Lot Of People Like That

IYQ = I like you

ILA = I Love Acronyms

ILU = I Love You

ILY = I Love You

ISS = I Said So

ISAGN = I See A Great Need

ISWYM = I See What You Mean

ISTR = I Seem To Remember

ITIGBS = I Think I'm Going To Be Sick

IWSN = I Want Sex Now

IWALU = I Will Always Love You

IBRB = I Will Be Right Back

I 1-D-R = I Wonder

I-D-L = Ideal

ID10T = Idiot

IIRC = If I Remember Correctly or If I Recall Correctly

IIR = If I Remember or If I Recall

IITYWIMWYBMAD = If I Tell You What It Means Will You Buy Me A Drink

IITYWYBMAD = If I Tell You Will You Buy Me A Drink

IIMAD = If It Makes An(y) Difference

IIWM = If It Were Me

INNW = If Not Now, When

IYKWIM = If You Know What I Mean

IYKWIMAITYD = If You Know What I Mean And I Think You Do

IUM = If You Must

IYSS = If You Say So

IYSWIM = If You See What I Mean

IBIWISI = I'll Believe It When I See It

ISYALS = I'll Send You A Letter Soon

IOH = I'm Outta Here

IPN = I'm Posting Naked

N-A-Y-L = In A While

IAC = In Any Case

IAC = In Any Case

IAE = In Any Event

IBTL = In Before The Lock

IBT = In Between Technology

IC = In Character

IMAO = In My Arrogant Opinion

IMCO = In My Considered Opinion

IMHEIUO = In My High Exalted Informed Unassailable Opinion

IMHO = In My Humble Opinion

IMNERHO = In My Never Even Remotely Humble Opinion

IMNSHO = In My Not So Humble Opinion

IMO = In My Opinion

IMOO = In My Own Opinion

INPO = In No Particular Order

IOW = In Other Words

IRL = In Real Life

ITM = In The Money

IYD = In Your Dreams

IYO = In Your Opinion

NDN = Indian or Native American

ISH = Insert Sarcasm Here

IOUD = Inside, Outside, Upside Down

IM = Instant Messaging -or- Immediate Message

IIIO = Intel Inside, Idiot Outside

I&I; = Intercourse and Inebriation

IDM = It Does Not Matter

GRRRR = it means Growling

<3 = it means: a Heart

404 = it means: I Haven't A Clue

143 = it means: I Love You

411 = it means: Info

BEOS = it means: Nudge

SUP = it means: What's Up

ISTM = It Seems to Me

IAITS = It's All In The Subject

INMP = It's Not My Problem

JAS = Just A Second

JAD = Just Another day

J/C = Just Checking

JDI = Just Do It

J5M = Just Five Minutes

J4G = Just For Grins

J/J = Just Joking

J/K = Just Kidding

JK = Just Kidding

JM2C = Just My 2 Cents

JMO = Just My Opinion

JOOTT = Just One Of Those Things

J/P = Just Playing

JSU = Just Shut Up

JT = Just Teasing

J2LYK = Just To Let You Know

JTLYK = Just To Let You Know

J/W = Just Wondering

KIT = Keep In Touch

KIR = Keep It Real

KISS = Keep It Simple Stupid

KMP = Keep Me Posted

KUTGW = Keep Up The Good Work

KPC = Keeping Parents Clueless

KBD = Keyboard

KIA = Killed In Action

KFY = Kiss For You

KK = Kiss Kiss

KOK = Knock

KWIM = Know What I Mean

LAQ = Lame Ass Quote

LSV = Language, Sex, Violence

LIFO = Last In First Out

L8R = Later

LOLA = Laugh Out Loud Again

LTM = Laugh To Myself

LBUG -or- LBIG = Laughing Because You Are Gay -or- Laughing

Because I'm Gay

LHO = Laughing Head Off

LIS = Laughing In Silence

LOL = Laughing Out Loud -or- Lots of Luck (or Love)

LOOL = Laughing Outrageously Out Loud

LOU = Laughing Over You

LTIC = Laughing 'Til I Cry

LWR = Launch When Ready

LMTCB = Left Message To Call Back

LMK = Let Me Know

LDTTWA = Let's Do The Time Warp Again

LHOS = Lets Have Online Sex

LMIRL = Let's Meet In Real Life

LONH = Lights On, Nobody Home

LBR and LGR = Little Boy's Room and Little Girl's Room

LKITR = Little Kid In The Room

LRF = Little Rubber Feet

LULU = Locally Undesirable Land Use

LD = Long Distance -or- Later Dude

LDR = Long Distance Relationship

LOPSOD = Long On Promises, Short On Delivery

LTR = Long Term Relationship

LTNS = Long Time No See

LLTA = Lots And Lots Of Thunderous Applause

LOMBARD = Lots Of Money But A Right Dick

LYB = Love Ya Babe

LYLB = Love Ya Later Bye

LYKYAMY = Love Ya, Kiss Ya, Already Miss Ya

LYMI = Love Ya, Mean It

LY = Love You

LY4E = Love You Forever

LYLAB = Love You Like a Brother

LYLAS = Love You Like A Sister

LYL = Love You Lots

LYWAMH = Love You With All My Heart

LYCYLBB = Love You, see You Later, Bye Bye

MorF = Male or Female

MM = Market Maker

M8 or M8s = Mate or Mates

MA = Mature Audience

MIHAP = May I Have Your Attention Please

MTFBWY = May The Force Be With You

MTSBWY = May The Schwartz Be With You

MTBF = Mean Time Between Failure

M4C = Meet for Coffee

MOTAS = Member Of The Appropriate Sex

MOOS = Member Of The Opposite Sex

MOSS = Member Of The Same Sex

MOTSS = Members Of The Same Sex

MSG = Message

MB = Message Board

MOTD = Message Of The Day

MUBAR = Messed up Beyond All Recognition

MYL = Mind Your Language

MYOB = Mind Your Own Business

MSNUW = Mini-Skirt No Underwear

MUSM = Miss You So Much

MIA = Missing In Action

MfG = Mit freundlichen Gruessen

MOP = Moment Please

MSMD = Monkey See Monkey Do

MITIN = More Info Than I Needed

MTF = More To Follow

MWBRL = More Will Be Revealed Later

MAYA = Most Advanced Yet Accessible

MHBFY = My Heart Bleeds For You

MKOP = My Kind Of Place

MLAS = My Lips Are Sealed

MMHA2U = My Most Humble Apologies To You

MTLA = My True Love Always

NAZ = Name, Address, Zip (also means Nasdaq)

NISM = Need I Say More

Ne2H = Need To Have

NIMY = Never In A Million Years

NM = Never Mind or Nothing Much

NCG = New College Graduate

NG = New Game

NUB = New person to site or game

N1 = Nice One

NTK = Nice To Know

NBIF = No Basis In Fact

NBD = No Big Deal

NIM = No Internal Message

NOFI = No Offence Intended

NP = No Problem

NRN = No Reply Necessary

NSA = No Strings Attached

N/T = No Text

NW = No Way

NOYB = None Of Your Business

NAB = Not A Blonde

NADT = Not A Damn Thing

NALOPKT = Not A Lot of People Know That

N/A = Not Applicable -or- Not Affiliated

NIMBY = Not In My Back Yard

NIMJD = Not In My Job Description

NIMQ = Not In My Queue

NMH = Not Much Here

NMHJC = Not Much Here, Just Chilling

NMP = Not My Problem

NN = Not Now!

NQOCD = Not Quite Our Class Dear

NSFW = Not Safe For Work

NTIMM = Not That It Matters Much

NTTAWWT = Not That There's Anything Wrong With That

N2M = Not To Mention -or- Not Too Much

N2MJCHBU = Not Too Much Just Chilling, How about you

NWR = Not Work Related

NYC = Not Your Concern

N/M = Nothing Much

NIGYYSOB = Now I've Got You, You Son Of a B*tch

NMTE = Now More Than Ever

NTYMI = Now That You Mention It

NIFOC = Nude In Front Of The Computer

NAK = Nursing At Keyboard

OOTC = Obligatory On Topic Comment

OCD = Obsessive Compulsive Disorder

OTF = Off The Floor -or- On The phone (Fone)

OTTOMH = Off The Top Of My Head

OTW = Off The Wall

OT = Off Topic

OBTW = Oh By The Way

OICU812 = Oh I see you ate one too

OMG = Oh My God

OML = Oh My Lord

ONID = Oh No I Didn't

ONNA = Oh No, Not Again

ONNTA = Oh No, Not This Again

OIC = Oh, I See

OUSU = Oh, You Shut Up

K = OK

OAUS = On An Unrelated Subject

OTOH = On The Other Hand

OTP = On The Phone

ODTAA = One Damn Thing After Another

14AA41 = One for All and All for One

MOMPL = One Moment Please

OOAK = One Of A Kind

OLL = Online Love

OMIK = Open Mouth, Insert Keyboard

OWTTE = Or Words To That Effect

OC = Original Character -or- Own Character

OOC = Out Of Character -or- Out Of Control

OOF = Out Of Facility

OOI = Out Of Interest

OOO = Out Of Office

86 = Out Of or Over

OOTB = Out Of The Box -or- Out Of The Blue

OTL = Out To Lunch

OAO = Over And Out

OMDB = Over My Dead Body

OTT = Over The Top

OBE = Overcome By Events

PITA = Pain In The Ass

PMFJI = Pardon Me For Jumping In

PMJI = Pardon My Jumping In

PTP = Pardon The Pun

P911 = Parent Alert

PBB = Parent Behind Back

PIR = Parent In Room

PAL = Parents Are Listening

PAW = Parents Are Watching

POAK = Passed Out At Keyboard

PTPOP = Pat The Pissed Off Primate

PNATMBC = Pay No Attention To Man Behind the Curtain

P2U4URAQTP = Peace to you for you are A cutie Pie

PIMP = Peeing In My Pants

PP = People

PIN = Person In Need

PONA = Person Of No Account

PM = Personal Message -or- Private Message

POSC = Piece Of Shit Computer

PIAPS = Pig In A Pant Suit

PO = Piss Off

P-ZA = Pizza

PBEM = Play By Email

PLS = Please

PWP = Plot, What Plot?!

POV = Point of View

PHB = Pointy Haired Boss

PND = Possibly Not Definitely

PS = Post Script

PANS = Pretty Awesome New Stuff

PDQ = Pretty Darn Quick

PTH = Prime Tanning Hours

P&C; = Private and Confidential

PEBCAK = Problem Exists Between Chair And Keyboard

PICNIC = Problem In Chair, Not In Computer

PIBKAC = Problem Is Between Keyboard And Chair

P2C2E = Process Too Complicated To Explain

PSO = Product Superior to Operator

PD = Public Domain

PDOMA = Pulled Directly Out Of My Ass

PMIGBOM = Put Mind In Gear Before Opening Mouth

POAHF = Put On A Happy Face

QQ = Quick Question

QL = Quit Laughing

QS = Quit Scrolling

QOTD = Quote Of The Day

ROR = Raffing Out Roud (in Scooby-doo dialect)

RBTL = Read Between The Lines

RMLB = Read My Lips Baby

RMMM = Read My Mail Man

RTFAQ = Read the FAQ File

RMMA = Reading My Mind Again

RL = Real Life

RLF = Real Life Friend

RSN = Real Soon Now

RT = Real Time

RTBS = Reason To Be Single

RX = Regards

RE = Regards or Hello Again

RC = Remote Control

RAT = Remote(ly) Activated Trojan

RFD = Request For Discussion

R&D; = Research & Development

R&R; = Rest & Relaxation

RTK = Return To Keyboard

RB@Ya = Right Back at Ya

RBAY = Right Back At You

RN = Right Now

ROTM = Right On The Money

RTTSD = Right Thing To Say Dude

RKBA = Right to Keep and Bear Arms

RGR = Roger

RPG = Role Playing Games

RYO = Roll Your Own

ROFL = Rolling On Floor Laughing

ROTFL = Rolling On The Floor Laughing

ROTFLMAO = Rolling On The Floor Laughing My Ass Off

ROTFLOL = Rolling On The Floor Laughing Out Loud

ROTGL = Rolling On The Ground Laughing

ROTGLMAO = Rolling On The Ground Laughing My Ass Off

SED = Said Enough Darling

SWAG = Scientific Wild Ass Guess -and- Software And Giveaways

SWL = Screaming With Laughter

STD = Seal The Deal

SWALK = Sealed With A Loving Kiss

STW = Search The Web

SHMILY = See How Much I Love You

SWIS = See What I'm Saying

CUATU = See You Around The Universe

CUNS = See You In School

CUL = See You Later

CUL8ER = See You Later

CUL8R = See You Later

CYL = See You Later

CYO = See You Online

CU = See You -or- Cracking Up

SYS = See You Soon

CYT = See You Tomorrow

SOI = Self Owning Idiot

SMAIM = Send Me An Instant Message

SMIM = Send Me an Instant Message

SMEM = Send Me E-Mail

S2R = Send To Receive

SOH = Sense Of Humor

SOHF = Sense Of Humor Failure

SNAG = Sensitive New Age Guy

SWAK = Sent (or Sealed) With A Kiss

SII = Seriously Impaired Imagination

SMH = Shaking My Head

SOT = Short On Time

SOTMG = Short On Time, Must Go

SU = Shut Up

SUAKM = Shut Up And Kiss Me

SUYF = Shut Up You Fool

SOMY = Sick Of Me Yet

SO = Significant Other (i.e., spouse, boy/girlfriend)

SITCOMs = Single Income, Two Children, Oppressive Mortgage

SOIAR = Sit On It And Rotate

SICL = Sitting In Chair Laughing

Sk8r = Skater

SHID = Slap Head In Disgust

ZZZ = Sleeping, Bored, Tired

C-P = Sleepy

SBUG = Small Bald Unaudacious Goal

SLIRK = Smart Little Rich Kid

SETE = Smiling Ear To Ear

SFETE = Smiling From Ear To Ear

SOOYA = Snake Out Of Your Ass

SNERT = Snotty Nosed Egotistical Rotten Teenager

SFAIAA = So Far As I Am Aware

STS = So To Speak

SWDYT = So What Do You Think

SWU = So What's Up

SEP = Somebody Else's Problem

SSEWBA = Someday Soon, Everything Will Be Acronyms

SLT = Something Like That

SBTA = Sorry, Being Thick Again

SCNR = Sorry, Could Not Resist

SFX = Sound Effects

SLAP = Sounds Like A Plan

SLAW = Sounds Like A Winner

S4L = Spam For Life

STM = Spank The Monkey

STYS = Speak To You Soon

SIC = Spelling Is Correct

SOP = Standard Operating Procedure

SRO = Standing Room Only

FGDAI = stands for Fuhgedaboudit -or- Forget About It

OZ = stands for: Australia

SAHM = Stay At Home Mom

SITD = Still In The Dark

STR8 = Straight

SorG = Straight or Gay

SME = Subject Matter Expert

SF = Surfer Friendly or Science Fiction

DWWWI = Surfing the World Wide Web while Intoxicated

TTFN = Ta Ta For Now

TAH = Take A Hike

TAP = Take A Pill

TC = Take Care

TCOY = Take Care Of Yourself

TAS = Taking A Shower

T@YL = Talk at You Later

TDTM = Talk Dirty To Me

TLK-2-U-L-8-R = Talk to You Later

TTUL = Talk to You Later

TTYL = Talk To You Later

TP = Team Player

TILII = Tell It Like It Is

TNA = Temporarily Not Available

TTS = Text to Speech

TGIF = Thank God It's Friday

TY = Thank You

TVN = Thank You Very Much

TYVM = Thank You Very Much

THX or TX or THKS = Thanks

TNX = Thanks

TXS = Thanks

TA = Thanks Again

TFN = Thanks For Nothing -or- Til Further Notice

TIA = Thanks In Advance

TGGTG = That Girl/Guy has Got To Go

TFDS = That is For Darn Sure

PU = That Stinks

TWIWI = That Was Interesting, Wasn't It

TAFN = That's All For Now

TLITBC = That's Life In The Big City

TTT = That's The Ticket -or- To The Top -or- Thought That Too

TEOTWAWKI = The End Of The World As We Know It

TLGO = The List Goes On

TPC = The Phone Company

TPTB = The Powers That Be

MWAH = the sound of a kiss

TANSTAAFL = There Ain't No Such Thing As A Free Lunch

TMTOWTDI = There's More Than One Way To Do It

TIAIL = Think I Am In Love

TOY = Thinking Of You

TSIA = This Says It All

TWHAB = This Won't Hurt A Bit

TFH = Thread From Hell

TLA = Three Letter Acronym

TNT = Till Next Time

TOPCA = Till Our Paths Cross Again

TTG = Time to Go

TBA = To Be Advised

TBC = To Be Continued

TBH = To Be Honest

2B or not 2B = To Be Or Not To Be

TK = To Come

TTBOMK = To The Best Of My Knowledge

TWIMC = To Whom it may Concern

TOM = Tomorrow

TIC = Tongue In Cheek

TNC = Tongue In Cheek

2NITE = Tonight

TOT = Tons of Time

2BZ4UQT = Too Busy For You Cutey

TDM = Too Darn Many

2G2B4G = Too Good To Be Forgotten

2G2BT = Too Good To Be True

TMI = Too Much Information

TQM = Total Quality Management

TSR = Totally Stuck in RAM

TFX = Traffic

TCB = Trouble Came Back

TM = Trust Me

TSRA = Two Shakes of a Rat's Ass

UPOD = Under Promise Over Deliver

UBS = Unique Buying State

USP = Unique Selling Proposition

unPC = unPolitically Correct

^URS = Up Yours

VFM = Value For Money

VC = Venture Capital

VBG = Very Big Grin

VBS = Very Big Smile

VEG = Very Evil Grin

VSF = Very Sad Face

VM = Voice Mail

WTB = Want To Buy

WTGP = Want To Go Private

WOMBAT = Waste Of Money, Brains And Time

WKEWL = Way Cool

WF = Way Fun

WTG = Way To Go

WTMI = Way Too Much Information

WX = Weather

WAMBAM = Web Application Meets Brick And Mortar

WB = Welcome Back -or- Write Back

WOOFYS = Well Off Older Folks

WNOHGB = Were No One Has Gone Before

WAI = What An Idiot

WAYD = What Are You Doing

WDYS = What Did You Say

WDYT = What Do You Think

WITW = What In The World

WTH = What the Heck

WWSD = What Would Satan Do

WYSIWYG = What You See Is What You Get

WYSLPG = What You See Looks Pretty Good

WE = Whatever

WYS = Whatever You Say

WYT = Whatever You Think

WIIFM = What's In It For Me

S^ = What's Up

WU = What's Up

WYP = What's Your Problem

WYRN = What's Your Real Name

WAYN = Where Are You Now

WTSDS = Where The Sun Don't Shine

WWY = Where Were You

WUF = Where You From

WC = Who Cares

WCA = Who Cares Anyway

WDALYIC = Who Died And Left You In Charge

WEG = Wicked Evil Grin

WG = Wicked Grin

WAG = Wild Ass Guess

WYCM = Will You Call Me

WISP = Winning Is So Pleasurable

WOG = Wise Old Guy

WYWH = Wish You Were Here

WDR = With Due Respect

WOP = With Out Papers

WRT = With Regard To or With Respect To

W/O = Without

WAD = Without A Doubt

WT = Without Thinking -or- What The -or- Who The

WTTM = Without Thinking Too Much

WIT = Wordsmith In Training

WIP = Work In Process

WFM = Works For Me

WIBNI = Wouldn't It Be Nice If

WIU = Wrap It Up

WBS = Write Back Soon

YA = Yet Another

YACC = Yet Another Calendar Company

YA yaya = Yet Another Ya-Ya (as in yo-yo)

U = You

UR = You Are

URAPITA = You Are A Pain In The Ass

URYY4M = You Are Too Wise For Me

URWS = You Are Wise

YAFIYGI = You Asked For It You Got It

YDKM = You Don't Know Me

YGBK = You Gotta Be Kidding

YHM = You Have Mail

YKW = You Know What

YNK = You Never Know

YTTT = You Telling The Truth

U2 = You Too

U-L = You Will

YBS = You'll Be Sorry

YEPPIES = Young Experimenting Perfection Seekers

YUPPIES = Young Urban Professionals

YCT = Your Comment To

YMMV = Your Mileage May Vary

YOYO = You're On Your Own

YRYOCC = You're Running on Your Own Cookoo Clock

YW = You're Welcome

YWIA = You're Welcome In Advance

YIC = Yours In Christ

Inspired by Netlingo.

INTERVIEWS & TESTIMONIALS

Here are some real life interviews and testimonials from some mothers and daughters. Enjoy!

Liz Martinez 53years & kristain Martinez 12 and a half

Liz: **Advice to a teenage girl:** It is not the outside that matters as much as building character from inside. They should follow the golden rule: think of others before yourself and chose Christ-like peers.

Find your child abused by relative? I will first pray, then confront, then seek professional help.

How different is raising teens compared to when you were one? Temptations are the same, but there is a prevalence of drugs and teenage sex becoming more pronounced and acceptable, or fashionable. Our teens are more desensitized to bad language, vulgarity, violence, and some have a difficulty discerning what is right or wrong.

Kristain: My worst fear in teenage years is growing fat!
I will not write the type of things teenagers get into!

Helen: Children should discuss everything with their parents. Some kids are scared of their parents.

My Daughter just said she is pregnant, my reaction?
I don't know..I would be shocked, she is not married, and I would be devastated. I would be angry, I would be disappointed, but I would be careful so she does not try to abort it. She has to keep it. I won't give the baby out for adoption. She has to go finish school and make promises it would never repeat itself..

Alice: I sometimes think she is interfering, I guess it's for my good. But it sometimes comes off as she does not trust, or pressuring me. I have got some education from friends than from parents, but if there are issues I want to clarify, I ask them. It's not stuff, they cannot discuss with me

If I find I am pregnant, I would discuss it with her, but she may not be the first person because I already know what she would say or her reaction. I would tell somebody else on the way to tell her

Dangerous practice: A lot of my friends say their parents don't know or are in denial that they are having sex.

Difference in raising teens as against when I was a teen? We were raised in fear, respect to revere our parents so there was a void or gap. We could not discuss things with them. Certainly not sex. Now, my daughter knows that even though I am first her mother, I am also her friend and we can talk about anything and I am always there for her.

I find Dayobomi pregnant? I would be very disappointed. First with myself, because I would feel I missed something. The signs must have been there, did I neglect her, why did I miss that? Was I too busy not to be observant of my own daughter? We watch 16& pregnant, the TV show together and we discuss it afterwards, so I would be quite disappointed that after seeing what those girls have to go through and my counseling, she follows the same path. But I would never ask her to get an abortion.

How do you view technology and the media? It's a demon! It's eating into our children, taking good quality time away from family time and teaching absolutely nothing. Dayobomi was recently grounded, and I don't recall for what, but the 3 months were the best time we have had as a family. We took away her telephone and laptop privileges and spent time bonding. It was great. As for social networks, well, they have to be monitored. There is nothing like privacy there. I have her passwords, I see everything going on there, and her friends are on my friends list. If I see anything inappropriate, that's it.

Advice for young girls? Don't be in a hurry. There is so much time to explore when you can deal with these things. Don't do things that you will regret for life. I tell my child, the name you are called in high school would follow you for life. People would refer to you as that girl who did... whatever. So don't do anything in a hurry or that you will regret.

On molestation of young girls: An uncle tried that with me, and I slapped him hard! He had no good intentions; I don't care what his relationship is. So no young girl should be scared. Beat, poke, abuse them and do not be intimidated.

DAYOBOMI: I sometimes feel she is violating my space, but I know it's for my good. I talk about anything, anything. I know she has my back. I don't allow peer pressure get to me, if they are doing things I shouldn't or feel comfortable doing, I let them go. There must be lots of girls or friends who they can be friends with, just not me.

Wardah Raja-Gyadenda

On Circumcision. I respect peoples view point. I have been where people differ strongly with strong points.

Mothers should discuss these issues: Menstruating should be discussed from young age, responsibility of a mother as nurturer and raising the self esteem, being well rounded and prepared for your multi-tasking role in motherhood.

Your thoughts on technology: I support it, but not against original talking. Imagine children talking with parents via text, it is different from talking to the child. We don't get the emotional aspect.

Your daughter tells you she is pregnant? I can't pretend because it will hit me hard. In Africa, some parents would kick the child out. It's an accident that changes people's lives and the people need moral support when such things happen as opposed to being ostracized. They start doing all sorts of things and we need support even by government. For those who have received support, they realize their mistakes and become support for others.

If you find that you are pregnant, would you tell your mother? I would tell her. I would sit her down and tell her the truth. There are some things that are just hard to keep from my mommy. The truth will hurt, but we will have to get through it together. **Do you get more education from the media than from your parents?** I got it from my parents. My parents taught morals and life lessons for growth, but teachers and some media taught me things that happen in school and core curriculum.

What age to start sexual education? It will depend on individual child. You can start if you find that a child is starting to have interest in boys or when they begin their period, and when the reach adolescent. My mother began, when I started my period.

What would you consider the most difficult subjects to discuss with your daughter & Why As a mother no subject should be difficult for you to discuss with your children. God has given them to you to raise and train. You have to just find the most effective way to discuss things with your children. Always use the word of God to guide you. The Bible is the master blue print for all we need to know.

What advice would you give a young teenage girl about life? Life is like a treasure quest hunt. You may not fully understand or find what you a looking, until you get to the end. My focus is the word of God that says, "For I know the thoughts that I think towards you thought of peace, not of evil, to give you an expected end. Jeremiah 29 v.11 Yes, I can be both friend and mother. They function at different circumstance. There is a place for parent to be a friend to their children. Just as Christ is our friend and our Father.

What totally freaks you out about the teenage years? Deviating from what I thought them, their peers influence.

Your teenage daughter just told you she is pregnant. What would your reaction be? Teenage pregnancy is because they are looking for care and love from parents. That is why parent should give their children 100% of their love, care and attention. Make time for them; do not put your job or other things before your children's need and future. Teach them the way they should go and they will not depart from it.

Do you find it uncomfortable to talk about sex or boys with your mother? Why? I do not really discuss sex with my mother. What she told me was, not to place myself in any situation with men, where I will be vulnerable. She thought me that sex has it rightful place in marriage. She stresses that when a young girl or boy focuses on boys/girls and sex, it always prevent them from moving ahead as the Lord plan for them. Our focus should be in God and our career.

Raising teens as a single mother. "I can advice mothers to keep teens very busy and occupied with all activities. It may stress you out, but it's worth it because it pays off. Get them involved in a local church and in community events, that way they meet other church kids and engage in wholesome activities. I also made them start working early so they appreciate making and balancing money with the realization that you cannot possibly get everything you set your eyes on. There are needs and there are wants. Getting children independent early is important. I had to sacrifice a lot of myself by making sure I did not have any relationship pr different men coming to my house so that the house was a safe sanctuary for them. I had to set that example. I don't think kids should be doing certain things too early. A girl of 14 has no business having a boyfriend. There is so much she needs to be doing. The media today like music, films send negative messages to teenagers, hanging around the wrong crowd, and having any idle time is bad for teenagers. The internet's negative influence in this time is so much. You have to really monitor and watch out so your child does not get to that point. You cannot watch them all the time, so the key is communication. A parent is first a parent, before a friend.

Paula: Too much freedom in the USA for teens. In India kids stay with parents till they are married. Here kids are sent out at an early age. At 18, they are still kids. I still watch mine, no matter the age, until marriage. I do not let them go to anybody's home for anything, sleep over's or whatever, because you cannot watch them. Here they do not even want you asking who will be there, the other friends or their families. So, I will not let my kids go anywhere I do not know all the parents. In India it has to be more of school work, book exchange etc. Many of my friends lose their children to this society and they are full of regrets. I am getting myself ready to accept that my daughter may not marry a Hindu. I will have to tell her what she is in for because she is raised Hindu, everybody in her family is Hindu, but all her friends are not Hindu. We do not eat certain things like eggs, coconut. It is a different culture and you can take the good, but leave the bad. I still believe in arranged marriages at least till you are a certain age like 25. It is a family thing and very revered. I was arranged and we have been married 20 years: we have different ways, but we respect each other. Maybe not for my daughter. These days, the TV does sex education. Even the cartoons are talking about relationships. I would not want to expose them too early or they will want to experience it. You should tell kids what mistakes you made as a mother and why you do not want them doing same because of the consequences. Parents should watch their kids when they start acting funny. You can see the signs.

Justina Dibua- Educator, mother

Some parents are hypocrites. They do not tell their children their children the truth about life and how growing as a teenager was also challenging for them. They make themselves seem the perfect "A' student and child. How will you your child learn that it is alright to falter and fail at some things and not feel discouraged? Parents have to be real. It is not surprising that teens look at us as Aliens. We don't seem to have the same weakness that they have! As a mother who has raised 6 teenagers, I can say the most important relationship to prevent alienation is one of openness, being real and honest with your kids and letting them know that you are human and can make errors too.

F: I heard about sex in 8th grade (14). Mom did not discuss it, I heard from friend, church & TV. It's easier to talk about it with friends.

It does not come up at my house. Maybe because my mom figures I already know.

A: It's awkward when I hear girls talking like that. I stay away from such people.

F: There is pressure to be the "in' girls. But that is part of teenage life and growing up. The "in" crowd does all the crazy stuff and asks questions like"oh, how was your weekend? I did this and that...what did you do?" They see the things they do as having fun...well, the fact that you are not pregnant yet, does not mean it cannot happen. I do not go to certain parties with some people because I have no interest. The cops always come to break such parties up, there is drugs, sex, alcohol and you always hear that something goes wrong. Why do you want to go? I will not go. When it comes to the social networks, people are not aware that things do go wrong by adding the wrong friend to your list of friends. They just think, "Oh, he looks cool. I'll add him" and you really have to be at a level of maturity to operate these internet tools. You do not know if he is a predator posing.

A: Yes, some 40 year old guy can pose as an 18 year old and they ask you to meet them. It's just lacking of good judgment.

F: Yes, would you go to a stranger off the street and divulge all your personal information to him, so why would you do that on the internet?

It's totally poor judgment. Then they ask you to meet them, and you go...I mean why would you even do that?

F: Sexting is so stupid...sending pictures naked, showing all sorts and sending on phone and when girls do that to guys, he is usually with some buddies, showing them and they are having such a good laugh, and they forward to each other and soon the girl is all over the place and it's so embarrassing.

A: It's terrible and they do it without thinking about what would happen. It's worse because they do some of these things when they are together and when they break up, the boys splashes it around. Some things we do now can come back to hound us in the future

F: Its more girls than guys that do it. Boys that do that are so creepy. In terms of safety, I'd say be around the right people because even if you don't do some of the things, just being around those people can get you in trouble. Go in a group when it comes to dating, that's what my mom says. When you are in the right group, it's a lot more difficult for one boy to tell you to try stuff. Also think about what you want to do before you do it. Pay attention to the news by being current about things and situations that have happened to other girls, have fun, but not too much because that is how it starts.

A: I think you have to think of where you want to be and the price you may pay for your act. Young girls, my age, who have dropped out of school from teenage pregnancy end up never going to finish in school, they do not get their diplomas, go to college and they end up not being able to care for themselves,.

F: Body Image: It's a big deal: girls listen to what boys tell them, boys get ideal images from models and TV. It's so not real. Girls try all sorts of things you know, binging, dieting, and try not to gain any weight. The models look sickly and skinny and they do not look healthy. I believe you have to be comfortable with yourself. A: especially when she is trying to get a boyfriend. The TV says you have to be this height to be pretty.

F: .My parents are old fashioned about sleep over's. Can I just go to their house and you trust my judgment? I mean, you cannot possibly know everyone in a sleep over party.

A; Yes, it can be aggravating particularly when they have talked to you and have taught us to have better sense so it's like they don't trust you.

F: We have to think about choices. It's important. We cannot be fun loving all the time and we have to do the tough stuff now and have fun later.

Dr. Josephine Ediale: I had concerns about their early exposures to things like pornography, homosexuality, total lack of morality, exposure to boys among their peers. I try to be a role model because children are great copy cats. It's more about what they see me doing than what I tell them. They also have to know who they are and be comfortable with it. I tell them we all have different background, different family values. I make sure they know about our cultural differences and how we were raised. I believe if you bring God into it and let them know that they are special to God and these are God's rules and ask them to abide by it, it makes life easier.

When I was growing up, things were kept secrets but now children want to know about things and if you don't tell them, they will find out anyway and from the wrong source. Nothing is too big and I am pretty open. If it's not open, they may be misled.

Ehi & Ofure Ediale:

Ofure: Yes, mom is pretty up front with a lot of things. I can't believe she was not raised like this! She discusses anything with us and because we spend a lot of time researching and reading, we come upon these topics often. Maybe being a doctor helps

Ehi: We ask questions about other areas as well, like economics, sciences, arts and because of their open manner of dealing with other areas, it does not seem a big deal. We just know that there are things that are age- appropriate and right now, we need to focus on the right things for our age. It is wrong in God's eyes, so why do it?

Josephine: I have read this manuscript with my daughters and there are areas that even as a doctor, I was unaware of, so I have learned a lot from it. And I guess, reading it with them makes it more interactive and informative. It's a great book for young girls and mothers too!

The big difference between when I was raised and now is social media and the devastating effects it has on girls. Read the headlines. Suicides over cyber bullying. Pedophiles stalking on the internet. Suggestive pictures to/from boyfriends & girlfriends leading to child pornography charges or becoming public property. Reputations ruined by one innocent error or one wild moment. When I was a kid if you made a stupid decision (which everyone did) maybe you only knew or had a couple of witnesses, now it could end up on the internet for eternity.

My biggest fear in raising my 2 daughters is the society in which we live. We live in a post-Christian society which values what you have and what you look like above who you are. We live in a society with a constant barrage of social media (texting, cell phones, blogs, etc). Girls must be more vigilant than ever to guard themselves against exploitation not just from adversaries but from well-meaning friends as well. Also, we have a constant flow of communication/ entertainment. Kids aren't taught to go amuse themselves quietly. Kids need to be able to be quiet and hear God's voice.

The biggest advice on life is staying grounded, focusing on education, health and spirituality. Self-esteem and confidence will go a long way during your teenage years and beyond,

As a teenager, you will experience a lot of "Big Firsts" like first crush, first part-time job. Enjoy your teenage years; don't be in such a rush to become an adult. Once your teenage years are gone, they become just memories. Make the best memories ever by being the best you can ever be.

There is a limited amount of control parents have on what your teenager is exposed to. My remedy to this is becoming "best friends" with my daughters and having making myself available to them at all times and having open discussions with them (no matter how trivial). Hopefully, we will be "BBFs" (best friends forever).

Mothers, make yourself available to your daughters at all times. Teenage years are the most difficult for our daughters, we need to be there with and for them, guiding and loving them through it all and being supportive, even when they err. Chastise when necessary but always love them no matter what. According to the old Nigerian adage, "use your right hand to punish a child that has wronged and the left hand to pull him/her back to you". Hopefully all the words of wisdom you share with them will not depart from them and will help influence the decisions they make when you are not around.

Susan Laurence, 39   Girls age 7 and 5

Girls are more hurtful to one another at an earlier age. When a girl gets upset, they say mean words to their "friends" such as "I am breaking off our friendship, you are not invited to my party" or make fun of their appearance. They are very competitive at an earlier age. I continually hear little girls say that they are better than their friends at a sport, coloring, singing, dance, etc. The tone that they use is very harsh. Plus the inappropriate words children say now at an earlier age is very alarming. I have to discuss these words with my daughters when they come home from school because someone in their class has said it and they want to know what it means. I need to discuss issues I faced, about 5 years earlier with my daughters then when I had to deal with it.

If I find my child has been sexually abused by a known person, first, I would make sure that my daughter knows that she did not do anything wrong and that she did the right thing by telling me. I would reassure her how much I love her and that I will take care of and protect her.

Then I would get her into a safe environment away from the abuser. I would then confront the abuser away from everyone. If they deny the abuse, I would have them take a lie detector test to verify their statement. If they are found to be lying I would press charges. As a parent it is my responsibility to protect my children, even if it means going against another family member.

As for the pregnancy, I would allow for my daughter to have an abortion. I am for pro choice when the situation involves rape or abuse. Otherwise I believe in pro life. I would have my daughter start seeing a therapist to help her deal emotionally, physically, and mentally with the situation and learn how to move forward. Every step of the way I will be there for my daughter.

The biggest challenge in raising daughters is teaching them how to think critically, live by a moral code driven by what is right - not by what is simply acceptable by their peers, accept they are part of something much greater than themselves. Their dependence on the social media as a means to feel connected is so different from the social connections I had as a kid. I haven't yet seen them demonstrate the amazing power the Internet and other forms of technology can have on social change and education, so I would say, get an education, stay connected to the workforce even if motherhood is your calling, learn how to balance needs versus wants, learn how to change your own tire, and how to balance a checkbook. Another add - Do not let your relationships with boys define your self- worth and have your family's back - always.

I am a mother of five (5). Four girls (4) girls and one boy, the baby. My girls range from ages 18-23yrs now.
I always tell my girls to remember that I was once their age and that I am not their enemy.

My advice to my girls is that they should be wise and that if they chose to date,

1) To date someone that is a little older (3-5yrs older) than them. Reason being that women grow mentally faster than men from my experience.

2) The person must be more educated.

3) Must treat them well and respect their opinion

4) Not overly jealous

5) Respect their parents

6) Must not give money to any boyfriend. This may seem hash, but if you do, you are setting yourself up to be used.

7) Most of all, have the fear of God in them, in whatever they do.

You should be a parent first and foremost and then your child's friend. In today's world children have lots of friends and yes I have seen parents who are friends first. To me that's sad, these kids have no one to tell them what is wrong or right. I am striving to raise responsible, dependable children who grow into people who are an asset and contribute to their community. Look them in the eye so they know you can never be too busy to paint toenails, do mud masks or talk about books. These mundane things create a bond that will deepen and grow. Touch your children constantly! Give hugs, kisses and small touches throughout the day! Kids know without words then that you love them. Let them know you hold them close to your heart physically and emotionally! Nothing, nothing feels better than a mother's hug or touch!!

Stephanie: My mom is always asking questions: she wants to know everything I am doing, where I am, where I am going. I have to account for every minute of the day and sometimes it goes overboard. She does not watch over my older brother like that! Why me? I know she loves me. She does not want me to get hurt, but I have heard that so many times, that it is impossible not to remember it.

Pat: I am not first her friend. I am her mother. She must do the right things and I will not watch my daughter go astray. Of course I monitor her, but we sometimes have fun times together. My daughter can cook, clean, she is a good child and it is because she has been raised well. There are still challenges, but God will see us through. For now though, I am her mother first.

The world has convinced girls that they have little value if they have never had a boyfriend or a sad story about heartbreak to share. I know that girls today are uncertain, insecure and unable to get past this relationship/loneliness issue when so many of their peers have paired off. Find out how you are wired, find out what you love to do (besides flirting) and develop interests apart from dating. Your happiness in life is not dependent upon what a boy thinks of you!

When I was a teen, I was blessed to have a great youth ministry that provided many opportunities for us to hang out and grow spiritually. We were not encouraged to date and pair off so we had many happy, oblivious hours of being together as a group of kids who loved God and wanted to be involved in ministry.

A girl must guard how much she shares on social networking sights, how much she reveals to people about her heart and feelings, and avoid being alone with people she does not know.

References

2008 Report on the global AIDS epidemic. (n.d.). *UNAIDS: The Joint United Nations Pro- gramme on HIV/AIDS.* Retrieved August 14, 2010, from http://www.unaids.org/en/ KnowledgeCentre/HIVData/GlobalReport/2008/2008_Global_report.asp

2007 Face of Global Sex report. (n.d.). *Durex Network.* Retrieved August 14, 2010, from www. durexnetwork.org/en-GB/research/faceofglobalsex/Pages/Home.aspx

About Health - Alcohol: Feeling peer pressure. (n.d.). *About Health - "Real kids, smart choices, grow up."* Retrieved August 14, 2010, from http://www.abouthealth.com/t_topicX. htm?topic=25

Alcohol is linked to high blood pressure, cancers and heart attack. (n.d.). *Alcohol is linked to high blood pressure, cancers and heart attack.* Retrieved August 14, 2010, from http://www. drinking.nhs.uk/

Carolyn Janet Crandall, M.D., F.A.C.P. - MedicineNet - Health and Medical Information Pro- duced by Doctors. (n.d.). *MedicineNet - Health and Medical Information Produced by Doctors.* Retrieved August 14, 2010, from http://www.medicinenet.com/script/main/ art.asp?articlekey=12011

Check Yourself: A place for teens to check where they are with drugs and alcohol. (n.d.). *What are the Effects of Drug and Alcohol Abuse? | CheckYourself.* Retrieved August 14, 2010, from http://www.checkyourself.org/ShowRealStory.aspx?storyId=b0935c9d-aff4-4ae5- 93ee-752b1dc27026

Devitsakis, N. (n.d.). Peer Pressure. *Girl Power - Empowering Girls Worldwide.* Retrieved August 14, 2010, from http://www.girl.com.au/peer_pressure_yoursay.htm

Download Zone. (n.d.). *Oracle ThinkQuest Library.* Retrieved August 14, 2010, from http:// library.thinkquest.org/3354/Resource_Center/download.htm

Global patterns of mortality in young people: a systematic analysis of population health data: The Lancet. (n.d.). *TheLancet.com - Home Page.* Retrieved August 14, 2010, from http://www.thelancet.com/journals/lancet/article/PIIS0140-6736%2809%2960741- 8/fulltext

Info on Alcohol and Resisting Peer Pressure | The Cool Spot. (n.d.). *Alcohol, Peer Pressure and Underage Drinking Info for Young Teens | The Cool Spot.* Retrieved August 14, 2010, from http://www.thecoolspot.gov/right_to_resist.asp

Main Menu. (n.d.). *Oracle ThinkQuest Library.* Retrieved August 14, 2010, from http://library.thinkquest.org/10631/main.htm

Option Line Â» Considering Abortion. (n.d.). *Option Line.* Retrieved August 14, 2010, from http://www.optionline.org/questions/considering-abortion/

Philips AVENT - Breastfeeding & Feeding Baby. (n.d.). *Philips AVENT - Breastfeeding & Feeding Baby.* Retrieved August 14, 2010, from http://www.avent.com/

Sexually Transmitted Diseases (STDs) in Women: Causes, Symptoms, Diagnosis and Treatment on MedicineNet.com. (n.d.). *MedicineNet - Health and Medical Information Produced by Doctors.* Retrieved August 14, 2010, from http://www.medicinenet.com/sexually_transmitted_diseases_stds_in_women/article.htm

Staying Safe. (n.d.). *Staying Safe.* Retrieved August 14, 2010, from http://www.stayingsafe.org.uk/read-the-report

[ARCHIVED CONTENT] Independent Advisory Group on Sexual Health and HIV: Department of Health - Public health. (n.d.). *- The European archive: Collection page: European Archive.* Retrieved August 14, 2010, from http://webarchive.nationalarchives.gov.uk/+/www.dh.gov.uk/en/Publichealth/Healthimprovement/Sexualhealth/Sexualhealthgeneralinformation/DH_4079794

Pregnancy, t. f., & from, t. p. (n.d.). Female hormones. *NetDoctor.co.uk - The UK's leading independent health website.* Retrieved August 14, 2010, from http://www.netdoctor.co.uk/womenshealth/features/hormone.htm

Prevalence of Sexually Transmitted Infections and Bacterial Vaginosis Among Female Adolescents in the United States: Data from the National Health and Nutritional Examination Survey (NHANES) 2003-2004,

APA formatting by BibMe.org.

Other books by the Author:

N'OGBAISI-"THE CAGED LEOPARD"

AN AFRIMEDIA PUBLICATION

TRAGEDY OF BINI KINGDOM

WRITTEN BY
Eve Ikuenobe-Otaigbe

N'OGBAISI-"THE CAGED LEOPARD"

Eve Ikuenobe-Otaigbe

N'OGBAISI

Despite stern warnings, Ralph Moor and his troop with permission from Queen Victoria, invade the ancient ancestral city of Bini during a solemn traditional festival, and the enraged chiefs confront the party. This explosion leads to a military expedition against Bini with fierce fighting, bloody massacre and annihilation of the hapless natives and the subsequent capture of the city. The all-powerful monarch, Oba Ovonramen mysteriously disappears. With the uneasy calm, the British demand for the Oba's return to face court trials. Failure to comply would lead to such a violent carnage as never seen before.

This historical epic based on true events of West Africa in the 19th Century, projects the dubious and systematic take over of Bini Kingdom by the British merchants, who cart away prized historical possessions, ivory tusks, bronze statues and human resources as a fall out of this mayhem.

There is only one remedy by the colonialist rule: The Oba must be deposed and Queen Victoria imposed.

BIO

Eve is a Theatre Arts graduate with an impressive track record as a stage performer and Theatre Director. This multi-talented award-winning film director is also a published author of many works in varying genres and her works have received rave reviews, accolades and recognition world wide.

She is President of Afrimedia Entertainment and Founder of the American Arts Academy. She is also a member of the Public Relations Society of America and a member of Women in Films & TV, Atlanta, Georgia where she resides with her husband and four children.

http://www.afrimedia.org. E-mail: info@afrimedia.org.

ISBN 978-0-595-45328-3

$19.95 U.S.

iUniverse

www.iuniverse.com

51995

9 780595 453283

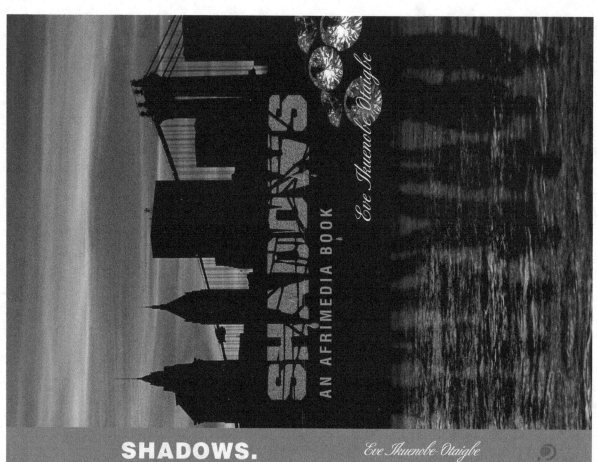

Tangled
An Afrimedia Book

Eve Ikuenobe-Otaigbe

Tangled   Eve Ikuenobe-Otaigbe

TANGLED....

...Beautiful Onyinye had great dreams for the future; to one day go to medical school and alleviate the suffering of her family.

Nduka, her brother who the family pinned their hopes had left for the US for medical studies. He marries Mia- an American and is faced with culture shock. Onyinye's family disintegrates right before her eyes and she contemplates prostitution to provide for her family.

She finds true love in Ifeanyi and just as her life starts to come together, her world is shattered by one tragic event after another.

....Will Onyinye and her family survive the hammering assault of societal dictates and values against the intense personal struggle of change and pleasure.

"A thought-provoking, gripping, intense and thoroughly enjoyable piece of storytelling..."
—*Publisher, Catalyst Magazine*

"Intriguing masterpiece characterized by interplay, twists so vividly portrayed and compelling...extremely informative and culturally insightful..."
—*Cleo Johnson-McLaughlin,*
President
Black United Fund of Texas

"Exceptionally engaging piece of work that embraces all aspects of humanity; from suspense to humor, empathy to sadness, a mixture of emotional conflicts..."
"...Spellbinding..."
"...Stroke of genius..."
"...Unraveling..."
"...Captivating; absolutely heart wrenching..."
—*Reader's comments*

Eve is a Theatre arts graduate with post-graduate studies in Mass communications. An accomplished playwright, theatre director and actress. She has various soaps, stage productions and films to her credit and resides with her husband and children in the United States.
www.afrimedia.org

$10.95 U.S.

iUniverse®
www.iuniverse.com

ISBN 0-595-31353-1
9 780595 313532
51095

THROUGH MIST

Vol 1

Eve Ikuenobe-Otaigbe

"Through Mist Vol 1" is an emotionally captivating, enthralling, commanding authentic blend of poetry and rhythm. The words are sensual, rousing, commoving and riveting; so vividly and flawlessly written with fluidity and style of excellence.

Pieces like *"Lafemme Africaine"* the African woman of color, *"Man the Eagle"* a potent generative proud piece on being a real man, *"Lines of Steel"*, a poem for the troubled youth, *"African"* a pride-filled cultural piece depicting constant conflicts of being African and American, *"Wishful"*, a surreal spiritual dirge for loved ones captured in ways only imagined but felt when read.

This book is a break-through in the phonology of words succinctly strung together. It heralds and signals a new depth and dawn in poetry.

Award-winning film director, dubbed "A generational barrier breaker" by SAIF and touted as "One of the emerging female writers of the decade"—NBAF, acclaimed author of works including *Tangled, Shadows, The Caged Leopard-N'ogbaisi* and more, **Eve** is a prolific fire-brand theatre director who has performed extensively on stage, TV and film, world-wide.

She is President of Afrimedia Entertainment, a Georgia-based Company and Founder of the American Arts Academy. A member of Women in Films, Georgia, Eve is married with children.

$18.95 U.S.

iUniverse

ISBN 978-0-595-45366-5

51895

9 780595 453665

www.iuniverse.com